HAPPINESS MATTERS!

21 (Thoughts That Could Change Your Life)

DENNIS LEONARD

Unless otherwise indicated, all Scripture quotations are from the *New King James Version* of the Bible, copyright © 1979, 1980, 1982, by Thomas Nelson, Inc., Nashville, Tennessee.

Scripture quotations marked NASB the *New American Standard Bible* © 1960, 1973 by The Lockman Foundation. All rights reserved. Used by permission. (www.Lockman.org)

Scripture quotations marked KJV are from the authorized *King James Version.*

Scripture quotations marked NIV are from the *New International Version of the Bible,* copyright © 1973, 1978, 1984 by International Bible Society, Colorado Springs, Colorado.

Happiness Matters!: 21 Thoughts That Could Change Your Life

Dennis Leonard
9495 East Florida Avenue
Denver, CO 80247
(303) 369-8514
www.DLministries.com

ISBN 1-880809-63-X
Printed in the United States of America

Legacy Publishers International
1301 South Clinton Street
Denver, CO 80247
www.legacypublishersinternational.com

1 2 3 4 5 6 7 8 9 10 / 09 08 07 06

DEDICATION

I dedicate this book to the spiritual leaders in my life...

Jesse Duplantis...thank you for teaching us to laugh and how important happiness is.

John Maxwell...thank you for teaching me the principles of success and the power of teamwork.

Bishop Paul S. Morton, Sr.,...thank you for believing in me when very few people did.

Bishop T.D. Jakes...thank you for teaching me to deal with my personal issues so I could walk in happiness.

And finally, I would like to extend thanks to Rick Warren for teaching me about purpose, which has changed the face of our church.

CONTENTS

INTRODUCTION

Happiness comes of the capacity to feel deeply, to enjoy simply, to think freely, to risk life, to be needed.

Storm Jameson

The mere mention of the word "happiness" creates in us a desire for all kinds of pleasurable experiences: joy and ecstasy, peace and contentment, satisfaction and fulfillment. And it is interesting that *Webster's Dictionary* just happens to define happiness as "a state of well-being and contentment: JOY...a pleasurable or satisfying experience."[1] Just think about it for a moment. Happiness is an amazing state of being.

Everything we do is about being happy, and happiness is a great motivator. It motivates us to achieve, to develop new inventions and ideas that will make our lives better, easier, and more enjoyable. Happiness motivates us to form families and build great communities. It will even encourage us to do something heroic in order to preserve the happiness of others.

On the flip side, every addiction we fall into is about finding happiness. Crimes are committed to possess things we believe will make our lives complete. And our desires to experience pleasure and satisfaction can get us into some incredible messes and even end our lives.

Whether happiness is a motivation for bad behavior or good behavior, it is obvious that it is very important to us. Why then, do we see so many people dragging through life, so encumbered and downcast that we wonder if they have ever known one moment of joy? Most people are obviously missing this great blessing of happiness.

I have found out that *Happiness Matters!* And as I have lived my own life, I have discovered some keys to finding and keeping happiness. I promise you that your life will be richer, fuller, and more satisfying than ever if you will take to heart these *21 Thoughts That Will Change Your Life*.

Thought 1

HAKUNA MATATA—DON'T WORRY, BE HAPPY!

Hakuna Matata! What a wonderful phrase.... It means no worries for the rest of your days.

Tim Rice

These are the words of Timon in *The Lion King*, an entertaining animated film that actually conveys a powerful truth: If you don't worry, you will be happy. When your mind and heart are consumed with hope, love, faith in God, and all the wonderful aspects of life you are happy. On the other hand, when you are obsessing about all the possible calamities and tragedies of life, that things might not work out the way you planned, and any moment life could take a difficult and painful turn; you are not a happy camper. You chew your nails anticipating people to be unfair, crazy, or cruel. Who knows what might happen in the next five minutes or the next fifteen years? There are so many things to worry about!

If that is you, you need to take Timon's advice! But in order to stop worrying, you first must identify what you are worrying about. What's got you down? Marriage problems? Do you worry about bad things happening to your kids or family? Perhaps losing your job, overwhelming debt, no money for food, a place to live, your kid's college education, retirement, health care, sickness, growing old…death?

All of these are significant concerns in our lives, but are they so significant that you lose your joy? And what about the "little, nagging worries"? You know what I mean! You have that big interview in the morning, so you're up all night worried the alarm clock isn't going to work. Or the car won't start, or you'll be late, will you say the right things?

We could go on and on, but I like what Erma Bombeck says, "Worry is like a rocking chair: It gives you something to do, but it doesn't get you anywhere."[1] And it certainly doesn't make you happy and your happiness matters.

The Antidote to Worry

Jesus said, "I give you a peace the world does not understand. Don't let your heart be troubled or afraid". When we know and love Jesus, we have peace; and with His peace deep inside, worry cannot invade our lives. We can enjoy an inner peace that is not shaken by any thought, care, or burden.

Jesus also told us that when we begin to worry we are to stop it immediately. "Let not your heart be troubled" means "STOP WORRYING!" We need to remind ourselves that in Him we have peace, and we do that by reading and meditating on His Word. My definition of worry is simply meditating on my problem instead of finding the answer to my problem in the Bible and meditating on the answer.

"Let not your heart be troubled" means "STOP WORRYING!"

The Bible tells us to meditate on God's Word day and night while the world tells us that it's normal to worry day and night. I choose what God says! There is something in His Word to dispel every worry. If you're worried about your kids, meditate on scriptures like Isaiah 54:13, "All your children shall be taught by the Lord, and great shall be the peace of your children."

As you meditate on the Word, Peter said, "Cast all of your cares on the Lord because He cares for you." Jesus loves you, and He wants to carry your burdens. So put your kids in His hands. He loves you and He loves your kids more than you do! Put every worry and fear in His hands. Trust Him to perform His Word and take care of you and your kids because you can't always be there but He can.

You say, "Oh Dennis, I come from a family of worriers." You come from a family of sinners too! The bottom line is to give it up to Jesus. Let it go and trust Him. Find out what the Word says about what's worrying you and meditate on that. Then Jesus will keep you in perfect peace.

Worry Is Deadly

Worry is more than something that steals your happiness. It is one of your greatest enemies. It will destroy you by stealing God's Word right out of your heart.

Worry is a thief.

"Wait a minute Dennis. You told me that the Word of God is mighty and powerful, and that it stands forever. How can worry steal it out of my heart?"

This truth is found in Mark 4:19, where Jesus said that the worries of this world would choke the Word of God and make it unfruitful. The Word is powerful, but if you don't stop worrying it will eventually cause the Word to be powerless in your life.

Worry is a thief. The enemy comes to steal the Word and get us worked up over our problems. He wants us to lose our peace and be miserable. He doesn't want us to be happy. He wants us to be paralyzed and neutralized by the cares of this world. He uses worry to steal God's best and blessings from our lives.

You must stop the thoughts of worry and meditate on God's Word instead; otherwise, the Word that was sown in your heart will be choked and will not benefit you. If you are believing God for a miracle in your life and give in to worrying, your worries will steal the Word that fuels your faith in God to perform that miracle. That is how deadly worry is.

If you love the Lord, then you need to know that nothing is impossible for Him. The enemy cannot stop the King of kings and the Lord of lords. If death couldn't stop Him, then nothing can stop Him. The only one who can stop Him from working in your life is you! When you worry instead of trusting Him, you choke His Word, kill your faith, and tie His hands. So let not your heart be troubled!

Strategies of the Enemy

The enemy will always remind you of your problems, trying to get you to worry. From the time you wake up in the morning until you finally fall asleep at night, he will whisper worrisome thoughts into your ear. You'll turn on a news program and see all the ways you could be robbed or murdered.

If the enemy can't tie you in knots worrying about your present situation, he will get you obsessing about your future—all the things that could go wrong in your life in…say…the next fifty years. I'm not saying that we don't plan ahead or set goals, but we get our plans and purposes from God and then we confidently go forward, trusting Him for our future.

Jesus said that God takes care of the birds of the air, so how much more is He going to take care of you? So quit worrying and trying to figure everything out! When you do that you are your own worst enemy because it is impossible for you to figure everything out. God is the only One who knows everything, so you must trust Him for your future.

Don't allow yourself to dwell in the enemy's land of worry, doubt, and unbelief. The last time I checked, God was bigger than any criminal who wanted to rob me and any mess that I got myself into. His angels don't go to sleep at night either! So rebuke every thought that opposes God's Word and kick that worry out of your life.

Pray Over Everything

Paul said to worry over nothing and to pray over everything. Whenever you encounter worry about something, you must pray, "God, I can't take care of this. It's too much for me. I put it in Your hands today."

It seems as though there are times in our lives that worry really comes against us with a vengeance. We will go through a period of time where we are nearly sick with worry about every area of our lives. Our minds are consumed with all the terrible things that might happen in a certain situation, and then we begin to worry about another situation—and another and another.

You have to make up your mind that worry is not going to get a hold of you. You can't help it if birds fly over your head, but you don't have to let them make a nest in your hair! You can't help it if worry comes against your mind, but you don't have to build a home for it there. You can pray through to victory.

> *"There is something about prayer that guards your heart and mind.*
>
> 

Prayer is a key to maintaining happiness because you turn from worrying to communing with God. You break the power of all thoughts of worry by turning your thoughts to His Word and trusting Him to perform it. Inner happiness is knowing God is on the scene, working on your behalf, no matter what is going on in your life.

There is something about prayer that guards your heart and mind. When you pray and give your worry to God, peace comes in the middle of the storm. He promises that if you will trust Him, He will give you a peace that will calm your stressed-out soul, a peace you cannot explain.

You will never overcome the worries in your life and be happy until you learn to give it to Him. I'm not talking about a mental game or going through some religious ritual.

I'm talking about talking it out with Him, giving it to Him, and letting Him change your heart and mind. Prayer changes you!

Prayer also takes situations out of your hands, which can only do so much; and puts them in God's hands, which can do anything. Prayer says, "God, I can't do it, but I know that you can." As you pray in faith, you are connected to the God who delights in doing the impossible, and all worry disappears in the midst of His presence and power.

Faith—or Control

Before you came to the Lord, you were in charge of your life. Now that you are a believer, He is in control, and you've got to learn to trust Him with every area of your life. In every situation, you will choose whether to handle it in your own strength and abilities or obey God and have faith in Him.

Having faith in God means that no matter what things look like, *you give up control of your life and put it in His hands*. You trust Him because He's your Father and He loves you. You know you are the apple of His eye, and He wants you to be happy more than you want to be happy. Remember, happiness matters.

Your faith in Him is not blind! Your faith in Him is based on who He says He is in His Word, and He is your Father. He will move heaven and earth to provide for you and protect you. This is an issue you must settle in your mind right now because if you don't believe God loves you and wants the best for you, you will not trust Him with your life. You will continue to try to control and manipulate your way into happiness.

Don't confuse control with personal responsibility. Personal responsibility is doing your part: praying, obeying, giving it to God, and trusting Him. Control is holding on to it and trying to manipulate everyone around you in order for things to go the way you think they ought to go. By doing this you are simply trying to be God. Giving your life to Jesus means giving up control. You cannot have faith in God and hold onto your life. Jesus said that those who lose their life in Him would find it, and those who hold onto their life will lose it. He knew that human beings hold on to things that they are not strong enough or wise enough to manage. Only He can keep us.

Every day I pray for my family and put them in my Father's hands, knowing that they are safer in His than in mine. I refuse to stay up all night worrying over what might happen to them. And I don't call them every hour to see if they are doing what I think they should be doing. I pray, I obey, I love them, and I have faith in God to keep them.

The real faith message doesn't mean you get everything you ask God for. *Real faith is believing and trusting God no matter what you get.* This can drive control freaks crazy!

But even if you lose everything you have, you have faith in Him to help you get it back, that He will give you double for your trouble.

Whatever is trying to bug you, just lift your hands to God and turn it over to Him. He will take care of it better than you could take care of it—better than you could ever imagine.

Don't Let Worry Steal Your Happiness

You can't even smile because the worries of this life have overtaken you. You can't enjoy a good meal because you're so uptight. You can't be happy because the worries in your life are choking the Word of God that gives you faith, hope, and peace.

If I'm describing you, then it is time to make the decision to stop worrying and get happy. It's time to give it all up to God and say, "If she leaves me she leaves me, but I will trust in the Lord, and I won't worry about it. If he takes all the money and runs off, Jesus will help me through it or straighten him out and bring him back better than before."

Maybe you are so worried about being single and alone that you go out with people that you know you shouldn't be going out with. You date people who are rebellious or even unbelievers. You are making decisions based on the worries in your life instead of basing them on God and

His promises to you! As a result, worry is keeping you from the mate God has for you.

The Bible says that anything that is not of faith is sin. (See Romans 14:23.) That means that worrying is a sin, and sin kills. God told us that whatever is not of faith is sin because if it's not of faith we are going to worry ourselves to death. We will make wrong decisions and might even miss His will for our lives. That's why He tells us the truth. He wants the best for us.

You need to declare, "I will fear no evil because He is with me. The Holy Spirit is in me. And the Creator of the universe is my Father and watches over me. He set His mighty angels around me and everything that concerns me: my family, my job, my ministry, and even the dog. I trust Him with my whole life." You just declared your freedom!

You know you have been set free from worry and are walking in faith when you get fired from your job and have His peace that everything is going to be all right. You know you are free from worry when people are talking about you behind your back but you still walk in love. You know you are no longer allowing worry to steal your life when folk hurt you and you forgive them and go on. You know you have soundly defeated worry in your life when all looks lost and you say, "My best days are still ahead. I am happy no matter what happens because my happiness comes from knowing the Lord." Happiness matters.

You don't worry when you walk hand-in-hand with the Lord. When you walk in the light with Him, the darkness of worry cannot grab hold of your soul and drag you into the pit of despair because your faith is strong. And as you walk with Him, if you listen carefully, I'm sure you will hear Him sing, "Hakuna Matata! What a wonderful phrase…". I'm not going to worry. I will be happy. Happiness matters.

To find more ministry tools go to:
www.HeritageChristianCenter.com.

Thought 2

FORGIVE OTHERS AND BE HAPPY

One of the keys to happiness is a bad memory.

Rita Mae Brown

Many people are terribly unhappy because they remember every single detail of every wrong that was done to them. Their minds are consumed with how this person betrayed them or that person lied to them. They spend much of their time being bitter, angry, deeply hurt, and even spiteful because someone offended them at some time in their recent or distant past. Without help, the only thing that will save them is a bad memory.

Unfortunately, most of us have great memories! But our natural tendency is to remember all the times we have been stabbed in the back and left in the lurch. That is why forgiveness is essential to happiness. Other than erasing our memories, the only way we can be happy is by forgiving those who offend and hurt us. You can't be happy as long as you hang onto your hurts.

The Good News

One of the most important principles in life is forgiveness. The Good News is that Jesus died for our sins so we could be forgiven by God and reconciled to Him. On the cross Jesus asked the Father to forgive those who put Him there—and we all put Him there. Now, as He forgave us, we are to forgive others. This is the Good News to all people.

If you live by forgiveness you will be happy.

If you live by forgiveness you will be happy. How does it work? God forgives you even when you don't deserve it. Therefore, He expects you to forgive others who don't deserve it. When you forgive, you act like God and forgive the unforgivable. By forgiving others you maintain a right relationship with God and with other people, which increases your happiness.

You will never truly be happy in this life as long as you hold onto a grudge or have a chip on your shoulder. If one of your goals in this life is to be happy, you must forgive people and let go of the hurt they have caused you. Quit talking about the things they did to you and talk to God instead. Tell

Him you forgive them and ask Him to forgive them. Turn them completely over to Him. Only then will you have peace in your heart and find true happiness and happiness matters.

Are Your Prayers Being Answered?

If you pray and pray and never get your prayers answered, you are not going to be happy. So it is important that you know how to pray effectively. Jesus said in Mark 11:25 that when you pray, make sure that you have forgiven anyone who has hurt you or offended you in any way. If you want your prayers answered, you have to let go of the past and forgive.

Our worldly nature or flesh is very unforgiving. But when Jesus Christ is our Lord, we are to put on His nature and forgive even when we don't want to. Preachers talk a lot about sins of the flesh like fornication and adultery, but none of these sins are as serious as the sin of unforgiveness. When we make up our minds not to forgive someone, we shut down our communication with God and close the windows of heaven in our lives. Our prayers will not be answered if we don't forgive.

Facing Reality

People hurt us. Sometimes they do it on purpose; sometimes they have no idea what they are doing. Sometimes folk are just mean and cruel. This is the reality of living with human beings on planet earth. To walk in forgiveness, you must be brutally honest with yourself at all times. Don't walk around like nothing is wrong if someone did something that made you furious or broke your heart. Take the mask off and admit you are hurt. Confront any unforgiveness in your heart and deal with it.

When you are in severe emotional pain, it is not easy to forgive people. That's when you just have to raise your hands to the Lord and say, "Help me, Jesus! Change my heart. Heal me." And I have found that as I pray for the person who has hurt me, slowly my heart begins to heal and soften toward them. I begin to see them through God's eyes instead of my own wounded heart. Then I am changed inside.

Another thing I do is go out of my way to be nice to them. When I see them, I just walk up to them and give them a hug or ask how they're doing. If their name comes up, I speak words of blessing over them. Walking in love cuts off the enemy's schemes and releases God's power into the situation.

Forgiving is walking in love, and you cannot harbor unforgiveness when you walk in love.

Just How Serious Is This?

If you never understand anything else in the kingdom of God, understand this: God is serious about you forgiving others. He is so serious that Jesus said if you don't forgive others, your heavenly Father would not forgive you! (See Mark 11:26.) Furthermore, you will never see breakthroughs, miracles, or be happy as long as you hold unforgiveness in your heart because your prayers will not be answered. Happiness matters.

The way you treat others is the way you will be treated.

You will always be unhappy unless you do things God's way. If you forgive others as our heavenly Father has forgiven you, He is free to bless you. In the kingdom of God, you have to forgive others or you cannot expect God to heal you, help you get a house, bring you a mate, or raise godly children. You must forgive for the promises of God to manifest in your life.

Sowing and Reaping

A principle that works with forgiveness is the law of sowing and reaping. The way you treat others is the way you will be treated. In Luke 6:38 Jesus said, "Give and it shall be given back to you, good measure, pressed down, shaken together and running over." Read this verse in context and you will see that He was not talking about money. He was talking about the way we treat others. When you sow forgiveness, you reap forgiveness. Sow unforgiveness, and you will reap unforgiveness—even from God.

Isaac was a great example of what happens when you walk in forgiveness. It was a time of famine, and he began to dig wells to find water. He would dig a well, and his enemies would come in and say, "That's our well." One day he began to pray for his enemies to be blessed. When he did, God caused his empty well to be filled with water.

God will cause the emptiness in your life to be filled with happiness if you will pray for your enemies, bless those who curse you, and forgive those who don't deserve to be forgiven.

Decide to Forgive

Spiritual maturity is measured by love, by the way you forgive. Anytime you get your feelings hurt or are offended even the slightest, you will decide whether you are going to hang on to it or forgive and let it go. If you want to grow up in God, you must start forgiving everyone for everything.

The Bible says, "Let all bitterness, wrath, anger, clamor, and evil speaking be put away from you, with all malice. And be kind to one another, tenderhearted, forgiving one another, even as God in Christ forgave you".

There are many ways we can tell if we are harboring unforgiveness toward someone.

- We think of someone and our blood boils or we get all worked up inside.

- We clam up and give someone the silent treatment.
- We continuously think or talk about what someone did to us.
- We constantly remind someone of what they did to hurt or offend us.

All of these things indicate that we need to choose to forgive someone. Remember the old saying, "When you point your finger at someone else, three others are pointing back at you, and your thumb is pointing up, reminding you that you need to be thinking, speaking, and acting like Jesus, who forgave you."

You can't help getting wounded, but you don't have to stay wounded. You can forgive, turn it over to God, and allow Him to heal you. You are in charge of your life, and no one can make you forgive. But no one can keep you from forgiving either! The decision is yours and happiness matters.

Forgive and Forget

Even as Christians, we tend to say, "I'll forgive you, but I'm not going to forget it." "Not forgetting" is just another way of rationalizing unforgiveness. It's a way to hold people hostage for the things they've done to us. We won't forget because we don't want them to forget it. We want to punish them for what they did to us. We want them to suffer the way we are suffering. But not forgetting only makes us unhappy. Happiness matters.

First, there are two things that God will not share with man. He will not share His glory, and He will not share vengeance. In Romans 12:19 the Bible says, "It is written, 'Vengeance is Mine, I will repay,' says the Lord." When you refuse to forgive and forget, you are seeking vengeance and usurping God's authority. This has serious consequences.

If you refuse to forget in order to punish someone or even try to get even with them, you separate yourself from God's presence. He will take His hands off of you. But if you forgive them, God will put His hands on them! Never pay back evil for evil! Trust God and watch how He works things out.

The second problem with choosing not to forget is that any time you hold something against somebody else, you are the one who becomes the hostage—to terrible oppression. Jesus told a story in Matthew 18 about a certain king whose slave owed him millions of dollars. The slave had no way of repaying the debt, so the king forgave him and cancelled the debt. That same slave had a friend who owed him a few dollars. He asked his friend to pay him what he owed and the friend said, "I don't have it."

Instead of showing his friend the same forgiveness that his king had shown him, the slave had his friend thrown in jail. When the king heard what had happened, he confronted his slave and said, "I forgave you of an enormous debt you couldn't possibly repay, but you did not forgive your friend of a small amount he could have repaid over a short period of time. Because you have done this, I'm turning you over to the tormentors."

Jesus illustrated that your debt of sin was so immense; there was no way you could pay it and satisfy God's just nature. Because He loves you—not because you deserve it—He paid it for you through His Blood. Now all heaven forgives you for eternity, even though you did nothing to deserve that forgiveness.

What that means for you today is that you have to forgive people who don't deserve to be forgiven as well. If you don't forgive others, you separate yourself from God's presence and place yourself in the hands of tormentors who keep you bitter, angry, and upset.

Dwelling on what your daddy did or did not do, how your boss doesn't pay you enough, or what your neighbor said last week will make YOU miserable, not them. The truth is, they probably don't have a clue they even offended you! You are the one in turmoil because you haven't forgiven or forgotten.

Not forgiving and forgetting ties you to the person who hurt you. You can't stop thinking about them. But why would you want to give them so much power over you? You can't stand them and want them out of your life. The irony is that the only way you can get rid of them is to forgive them and love them! When you choose to forgive and forget, YOU are set free. You can be happy when you forgive and forget. Happiness matters.

You Have to Forgive Yourself

It is hard enough to forgive other people, but sometimes it is even harder to forgive ourselves. This can work two ways. Sometimes we cannot forgive others because we have not forgiven ourselves. Sometimes we cannot forgive ourselves because we have not forgiven others.

You can be happy when you forgive and forget.

Have you ever met someone who has a hard time forgiving themselves for what they've done? It could be because they're getting back what they've sown. They have not forgiven others, and now they can't forgive themselves.

That may be you. Someone treated you badly in the past, and you have never really forgiven them and let it go. Now you have done the same thing, and you can't forgive yourself. *You cannot forgive yourself of something you have not forgiven someone else of doing.*

What if you cannot forgive others because you cannot forgive yourself? No matter what you have done, Jesus paid the price for it on the cross. "Dennis, you don't know what I have done!" Paul said he was the chief of sinners because he killed, tortured, and wreaked havoc among Christians before he was saved. But he forgave himself and so can you.

Pride says your sin is too great to be forgiven. You are saying that your sin is too big for the spotless Blood of Jesus Christ to wash away. You are exalting your sin above His Blood! And you won't be able to forgive anyone else of that sin either. So humble yourself and forgive yourself. Love yourself as God loves you. And forgive yourself as He forgives you. Then you will be able to forgive others of their sins too.

Eating Humble Pie Makes You Happy

It takes humility both to forgive people who have hurt you and to apologize to someone you have hurt. It is very hard to admit you are wrong or forgive someone else for being wrong because your flesh is proud. Do you know someone who always seems to have an issue with someone? They have an issue with their mother-in-law, their pastor, and even their dog. Show me a person who always has issues with others and you show me someone who is arrogant and proud. They are looking for someone to offend them so that they can point out how awful that person is, especially compared to their perfect self. Pride and unforgiveness feed each other, and they will make you very unhappy and eventually destroy your life.

Humility and forgiveness also feed each other. A humble person forgives and a forgiving person stays humble. The greatest example of humility is Jesus on the cross. Mankind had already ripped the skin off of His back and shoved a crown of thorns on His head. We had beat Him, pulled out his beard, and spit on Him. We stripped Him naked and made fun of Him. But He hung on the cross and cried, "Father, forgive them for they know not what they do." That is humility and forgiveness.

If you have any unforgiveness toward anyone, don't let another second go by without forgiving them. Right now you must humble yourself and forgive those who have ripped you apart, shoved you around, made fun of you, and had no regard or respect for you—just like Jesus did on the cross.

Remember, Jesus hung on the cross and forgave on Friday, but Sunday was coming! And you may be hanging on a cross today; but if you'll forgive all those who have hurt and offended you, it won't be long before your Sunday comes and a miracle happens! There is something about forgiveness that releases your pain and happiness matters. If you need further ministry, contact us at:

www.HeritageChristianCenter.com.

Thought 3

THE LOVE TEST

I believe that unarmed truth and unconditional love will have the final word in reality.

Martin Luther King Jr.

Love is the final word in all things. The universe was created in love by Love Himself. The Christian life begins and ends with love. God loved us so much that He gave His Son, Jesus, to die for us on the cross. His Holy Spirit wooed us with His love until we received Jesus as Lord and Savior, then Love took up residence in our hearts. There is no greater happiness than knowing the love of God.

Once we know the love of God, what happens? We have to pass the love test! We are to walk in love at all times and in all situations, to love as God loves. In this chapter I'm going to give you some things you need to understand in order to pass the love test and secure happiness forever.

1. If you don't have the love of God operating in your life, you are nothing. God says that even if you move in His power, have all the resources you need, and do all kinds of good works—but don't walk in love—your life is worthless. You can have all the money in the world, feed the poor, cast out demons, heal the sick, and even die a martyr's death; but if you don't love others the way God loves you, you are not living a good life.

Then He goes on to define love so you will know exactly what He means. He says, "Love is patient, love is kind and is not jealous; love does not brag and is not arrogant, does not act unbecomingly; it does not seek its own, is not provoked, does not take into account a wrong suffered, does not rejoice in unrighteousness, but rejoices with the truth; bears all things, believes all things, hopes all things, endures all things. Love never fails".

This passage of Scripture in First Corinthians 13, describes how you are to walk in love. Because love is a fruit of the Spirit, you can only do this by communing with Him. To operate in love and the fruit of the Spirit—love, joy, peace, patience, kindness, goodness, faithfulness, gentleness, and self-control—you have to cultivate a close relationship with the Lord every day. Only love gives meaning and value to your life and can make you happy. Happiness matters.

2. The enemy doesn't want you to walk in love because God's power works through love. Galatians 5:6 says that faith works by love, and 1 John 5:4 says that we overcome all the evil in the world by our faith in God. In other words, we must love for our faith to work. We cannot be jealous, unforgiving, arrogant, unkind, or rude and expect our faith to bring results. That's why the enemy goes out of his way to try to make us angry, upset, defensive, and uncaring toward others.

Only love gives meaning and value to your life...

You will not fall for the enemy's schemes if you follow this simple principle of the kingdom of God: It's all about Him not you. If you focus on what God is thinking and wanting instead of what you think and want, you are not only going to walk in love, but you will have great faith to defeat every obstacle. The key to miracles is great faith, and the key to great faith is great love.

How do you have power over your spiritual enemy? When he tempts you to gossip, say something nice about the person. When he tempts you to hold a grudge against someone, forgive them and go out of your way to be nice to them. You can rebuke the devil all day long, but if you don't walk in love, your faith won't work. And if your faith doesn't work, you will not be happy and happiness matters.

3. You were created to be an instrument of love and to bring healing to those around you. For coals to burn on a barbecue, they have to be joined together. If you separate a coal from the rest, its fire will go out and the overall heat of the rest of the coals is diminished. The same is true in the body of Christ. We were created to love one another and build the kingdom of God together.

Jesus said that the world would know we were His disciples because we loved each other. He prayed for us to become one in Him as He and the Father were one because that would be a witness to unbelievers that He was sent by God to be our Lord and Savior.

It's no secret that the enemy does everything he can to divide us. He knows that when there is unity, he is completely shut out. That's why we must refuse to be offended, forgive one another, and walk in love. Then we will not only be happy ourselves, but we will bring the joy of knowing God through Jesus Christ to others.

4. If you walk in love, you will not get offended. This is a simple but difficult fact. If you get up every morning with a commitment to love and forgive people no matter what they do to you during the day, you will never get offended. That means the moment anyone does anything to tick you off, hurt your feelings, offend your sense of justice, or injure you physically or any other way—you immediately make the choice to forgive them, ask God to forgive them, and turn the entire matter over to Him.

If you are offended, then you are not walking in love. In 1 John 4:20-21 God says that if you say you love God and you hate your brother, you are a liar. You cannot love God (who you cannot see) and not forgive or love your brother (who you can see).

There is no way around it. If you really love God you are going to refuse to be offended by anyone or anything. Remember, love is a choice not a feeling! You choose to love and you choose not to be offended.

5. Spiritual maturity is walking in love when your flesh is telling you the opposite. Spiritual maturity does not come with a degree in theology. True spiritual warfare is about walking in love when you don't want to walk in love.

In 1 Corinthians 13 Paul said that prophesying was good, seeing into the future was good, but none of these things are as good as walking in love. You'll never know true spiritual happiness until you make the decision to forgive people you don't want to forgive. You'll never grow up in Christ until you put on a heart of love.

You are not walking in love when you give someone the silent treatment for two days to punish them for what they did to you—no matter how many hours you spend praying. Repent for your unloving, unforgiving self; forgive the person who hurt you. That's walking in love, and that's maturity.

6. When you love people who don't deserve it, you love the way Jesus loves. God's love is unconditional. A human being's love is conditional. It says, "If you treat me the way I want to be treated, do what I want you to do, and meet all my needs, then I will love you. If you mess up or embarrass me in any way, I'm out of here!"

If we go by feelings, we'll always get offended.

I thank God that Jesus doesn't have that attitude. He told us and showed us how to live our lives. He said, "Love your enemies, bless those who curse you, do good to those who hate you, and pray for those who spitefully use you and persecute you". If somebody cuts you off in traffic, Jesus said to pray for them. When you hear someone is slandering you, Jesus says to bless her and do something nice for her. Why would He say pray for those that mistreat you? Because you cannot hate somebody if you're praying for them.

This is the love test, and we don't pass it by living by our feelings. We pass it by choosing to live by every word that proceeds out of the mouth of God. We can't go by feelings. If we go by feelings, we'll always get offended. God still has a work to do inside you if you know the Word, you go to church, but you are holding bitterness toward someone. Make the choice right now to love them the way Jesus loves you.

7. God cannot answer your prayers if you are not walking in love. Jesus told it like it is. He said in Mark 11:25-26 that when we pray, we must forgive, because if we don't forgive others, God won't forgive us or hear our prayers. I don't know about you, but I can't take any chances of not getting my prayers answered. I need too many miracles to be mad at you!

Unforgiveness is not the only sign that you are not walking in love. If you are arrogant and deceitful, ill-mannered and uncaring, or abusive and dominating toward people, do not expect God to answer your prayers!

Faith works by love, and if you are acting like the devil, treating others badly and disrespecting God's Word, your faith is going to be cancelled by your lack of love toward God and other people. If you want your prayers to be answered, you must crucify your flesh and walk in love.

Jesus is our example. He crucified His flesh on Friday and on Sunday resurrection power made Him alive from the dead. If you want resurrection power to answer your prayers, walk in love!

8. Stay fervent in your love for others because love covers a multitude of sins. There's no doubt about it. Church folk will get on your last nerve, but so can anyone in the world. Human beings have a tendency to rub each other the wrong way. The Bible has an interesting term for that. It's called iron sharpening iron!

The Bible says that if one of us is overtaken by a fault, we should go to them privately and restore them. We are also supposed to go with a humble attitude, because if we judge them, we will be tempted to do the same thing they did. That's passing the love test.

9. When you walk in love you don't condemn people when they fail. Some people do not have loving families, and they never will. Therefore, when they walk through the doors of a church they need to know that they are loved no matter who they are or what they've done. They need to know that they are in a safe place with people who will cover their faults instead of broadcasting them.

Jesus did not say they would know us by our denomination. He did not say they would know us by the size of our buildings. He said they would know us by our love. Talk is cheap. Anyone can say, "I love you. Of course I won't tell anyone." But how many really do love by keeping their mouths shut?

Remember, you have the power to change someone's life through love. When you reach out to unwed mothers, manage a ranch for troubled youth, visit prisons, or run a food ministry, you are saying, "I love you." And people cannot resist genuine love. They will go across town, spend money they shouldn't spend, and even get dressed up to be with people who love them.

10. We don't embrace all religions, but we love all people. True believers in Jesus Christ know that religion is mean. There's nothing loving about it. Your value and salvation are based on your performance. If you mess up, you are not only punished; you are damned. That is exactly opposite of being saved by grace through faith in the shed Blood of Jesus Christ. Christians know only Jesus can save us; we cannot save ourselves.

If you don't believe like some religions believe, they will kill you. Obviously there is no love in that. But Jesus came to show us God's love. He came to let us know there's a better way. That means there is no place for racism or bigotry in the Christian life. You will fail the love test if you hate people because of their color, nationality, religion, politics, or philosophy of life.

Jesus loves people from all walks of life and all corners of the earth. He died for everyone. Therefore, we cannot single out anyone because they are different from us or we don't agree with them and refuse to love them or treat them with respect. We must love all people as Jesus loves all people.

Love ignites faith to be saved, healed, delivered, and set free!

11. When love increases, demonic activity decreases. I have said this many times, but I will say it again. Spiritual battles are won and spiritual maturity is achieved when you pass the love test and love the unloveable, the unlovely, and the unloving. On the other hand, when love decreases, demonic activity increases. If love is not among us, you are going to see jealousy, envy, strife, contention, arrogance, pride, deception, and every evil work.

Faith works by love, and when love is gone faith is inoperative. I can't tell you how many times I've laid hands on somebody to be healed and God said, "Just put your arms around them and love them." Love ignites faith to be saved, healed, delivered, and set free! Where there is love, the enemy's power is neutralized and God's power is released for miracles.

If you want the presence and power of God to manifest always in your life, then walk in love. God's miracles will be released wherever you go.

12. You can't truly love as long as you're looking out for yourself. The nature of the flesh is to protect itself. "I don't know. If I forgive them, they might do this to me again." The greatest hindrance to loving others is self-centeredness and selfishness.

The reason some people are not team players and cannot seem to fit into the body of Christ is because their eyes are on themselves. It's all about them and their agenda. They will only play on the team if they can have it their way or are the center of attention. It is about their ministry and what God said for them to do. They haven't learned to walk in love.

The Bible says we are to put others before ourselves. And God has set the principle in His kingdom that by helping others accomplish their vision and calling, He will send others to help you accomplish your vision and calling. So take your eyes off you and look around. Take an interest in the people around you. Bless them, pray for them, and love them as God loves them. Then see what God will do in your own life.

13. If you don't know how to love, then draw closer to Jesus. There is a divine progression of love. The Bible says that we love God because He first loved us. First God loves us, then we love Him and others. You cannot love others without receiving God's love first.

If you are having a hard time loving people, especially those you need to forgive, then draw close to God. Let Him love you first and heal your heart. You can love, forgive, and have patience and understanding with others after you have received His love, forgiveness, patience, and understanding for you.

14. You don't have to feel forgiveness to forgive. Love is a choice and so is forgiveness. Neither love nor forgiveness are emotional in the kingdom of God. They are decisions you make to walk with God instead of without Him. Then you act according to your decision. You speak a kind word when you would rather give them a piece of your mind. You give a warm hug when you'd rather knock them in the head. That's spiritual warfare—and you are winning because you are passing the love test.

Bitterness opens the door for the enemy to come into your life. Forgiveness is walking in love and opens the windows of heaven for God's power to flow. God says, "If you want My help, drop the charges. If you want My healing, drop the charges. If you want to be in My will, drop the charges. If you want My favor to come on your life, drop the charges." Drop the charges and you pass the love test. You'll never be happy until you drop the charges.

15. "Vengeance is mine" says the Lord. What does that mean? The moment you try and get even with somebody, God will take His hand off of you. To pass the love test, you need to forgive your offender and turn the entire situation over to God.

Let me tell you something, you don't have to fight people who are against you. If you will have faith in God and walk in love, He will fight your battles for you. If you fight your own battles in the flesh, however, He will back off and you are on your own. I don't know about you, but that's not my idea of security!

Jesus said to love, pray for, and bless our enemies because that is being like our Father in heaven. It is no sweat to love our friends, but when they turn on us it is! Then, in order to pass the love test and be like God, we must choose to love them, forgive them, and turn them over to God. We never have to be concerned about defending ourselves if we walk in love.

When you are secure in God's love for you and then turn around and love others the way He loves you, you pass the love test and happiness is yours. Happiness matters. If you need more ministry materials to help you in your walk with the Lord contact us at www.HeritageChristianCenter.com.

Thought 4

ATTITUDE DETERMINES HAPPINESS

Most folks are about as happy as they make up their minds to be.

Abraham Lincoln

If you get your thinking right and keep a good attitude, happiness will come into your life and stay in your life. When you think positively you have a positive attitude, and as a result your whole life will have a positive charge. Even when you find yourself in the midst of a storm, you will be looking for the silver lining, the light at the end of the tunnel.

Thoughts form attitudes and attitudes determine destiny. This is a principle you must know and understand in order to secure happiness in your life. If you don't learn this, you will stay in the wilderness going in circles all your life, never making any real progress. You'll complain and complain—and wonder why things don't get any better.

The bottom line is that if you want to be happy—to walk in prosperity and health, see your children grow strong and become successful, and all of your family reaching their full potential—you must choose to have a great attitude no matter what the circumstances.

Who Do You Trust?

One of the saddest stories in the Bible is the story of God's people not going into the Promised Land. The children of Israel, who had been miraculously delivered from Pharaoh, missed out on all the blessings God had for them because they didn't trust Him over any situation or circumstance they encountered. Again and again in the wilderness they moaned and groaned at each challenge. Very simply, they had a bad attitude!

When it came time to go into the Promised Land, Moses sent twelve spies in first. Ten of the spies came back with a negative report. Only two, Joshua and Caleb, came back with a good report. Going by this standard, five out of every six people look at their problems and get a wrong attitude. Make up your mind that you're going to be the one who believes the good report and trusts God!

Whatever you are going through today, in order to maintain happiness you have to believe that God is going to get you through it. Are you reading this and thinking to yourself, *But you don't understand what I'm facing. All the odds are against me. I'm in an impossible situation!*

Maybe you'd like to own your own home but you have bad credit. Whether or not you are at fault, you can have faith in God to deliver you out of your mess and into your promise. That is a big attitude change, but with His help and by obeying His instructions you can do it.

One thing is certain, if you don't commit yourself to have a good attitude and trust Him over your circumstances, you'll be in the same place you are now in five and ten years. You'll never be happy or fulfill your God-given potential as long as you take the attitude that you can't trust God to overcome your giants.

Complaining Has Got to Go

Have you ever met somebody who complained about everything? Did it look like they lived a happy life? Probably not, because complainers are never happy! If that is you—if you know you're a complainer—you're going to have to make some changes in your thinking right now.

When something unpleasant happens to you, how do you react? Do you stop and look to God for the answer, or do you immediately give in to the emotion of the moment and become angry, frustrated, fearful, and furious? Developing the right attitude is learning to walk by faith and not by sight. It is finding your happiness in God instead of the situation in which you find yourself. And most important, it is learning to control your emotions and trust God.

In order to stop complaining you have to stop living by feelings and instead live by faith in God. If you live by feelings you'll be unhappy and do nothing but grumble. On the other hand, if you live by faith in God you will be happy and speak words of faith. I know that sounds too simple, but it really is just that simple!

Any time you see someone who is a winner, you'll always see that they have a great attitude no matter what is going on in their life. They don't sit around complaining about their difficult situation. When a challenge or obstacle comes their way, they just rise up on the inside and look to God for the solution—even if it looks impossible.

A great attitude is a secret weapon to see God move miraculously in your life. If you have an attitude of faith in Him and refuse to complain the possibilities for your life increase because all things are possible when you choose to trust Him over all the chaos swirling around you. Your good attitude keeps you hanging on when everybody else has quit, and that means you will win your race.

You Choose

Nothing ever just happens in your life, and that includes your attitude. You choose it. You choose to trust God and not to complain even when you don't feel like it. When everything around you falls apart, you declare, "I believe that no weapon formed against me will succeed. God is on my side and He will see me through to victory."

> *You and you alone are responsible for your attitude and your happiness.*

You and you alone are responsible for your attitude and your happiness. You cannot blame anybody else for having a lousy life or for being unhappy. Quit waiting for something or someone to change before you choose the right attitude! Decide right now that you are going to trust God for everything.

Say to yourself, "I may be in the wilderness today, but I'm coming out of it. This giant's not big enough to defeat my God!" Your choices are the only thing over which you have control. You cannot control other people or your circumstances, but God has given you full control over your will. You make your decisions, and your decisions frame your attitude—and your future.

We do not fail and become unhappy in this life because people don't like us, because we were born on the wrong side of the tracks, or because of our skin color. We fail and are unhappy because of bad attitudes. We simply refuse to put a stop to negativity, complaining, and excuses by making up our minds to have a good attitude.

It's not what happens *to* you that matters; it's what happens *in* you. It's not what people do to you that matters as much as how you choose to let it affect you. You must choose to keep the right attitude in spite of what you experience.

Every week I receive letters and email from people who tell me how much they love and appreciate me, but every once in a while I get a letter from somebody who just can't stand me. I have to choose, right then, to have a right attitude. I have to choose to look to God first for the truth about my life. Then I have to choose to love the person who wrote the letter and bless them, to not let their opinion keep me from what God has called me to do or who He has called me to be.

Choosing is simple, but it is not always easy! David had to look a giant in the eye and keep a right attitude. He declared to Goliath, "You come at me with a sword and a spear, but I come at you with the name of the Lord and this day He shall deliver you into my hands." The people of God thought that Goliath was too big to bring down, but David had a different attitude. He trusted God and thought, *this giant's too big to miss!*

Is Your Attitude Friend or Foe?

Your attitude will either be your best friend or your worst enemy. In fact, it does more than make you happy. Your attitude determines how far you go in every area of your life. It either draws people to you or pushes them away from you. It will influence your boss when the time comes to decide whether or not to promote you and give you a raise.

Doors always seem to fly open for the person with the good attitude. This is the believer who is looking to God and not to the world or their own abilities for promotion and blessing. That's the way favor works. When you put God first and have faith in Him, His favor comes on your life and you get promoted. On the other hand, if you trust in your own ability (which is limited) and have faith in your circumstances or other people (which are always changing), you tie God's hands. And He's the One who opens the door no one can shut.

Your attitude will take you to your potential or lead you away from your potential. That's why it is so important to develop a good attitude and keep it no matter what you hear, see, or experience. Make sure your attitude is your friend!

What Attitude Are You "Catching"?

Attitudes are contagious. That's why we have to be careful of the folk we hang around. If our friends have ugly attitudes then we will develop an ugly attitude. There's only one thing more contagious than a good attitude, and that is a bad attitude! Remember, birds of a feather flock together.

Show me your friends and I'll show you your attitude.

Show me your friends and I'll show you your attitude. Moreover, show me your friends, and I'll show you where you're going to be a year from now! Again, whom you hang out with is extremely important. Like Jesus, you can visit with those who have bad attitudes, but you must share your life only with those who inspire you to keep a good attitude.

If your friends are continually bringing you down, then you need to change your circle of friends. If they continually cause you to have a negative attitude and don't trust God, always "kind of hoping and thinking maybe" God might come through, then you need to find some new friends.

This is serious business! People with wrong attitudes are very difficult to deal with, and one rotten apple will eventually destroy all the apples in the barrel. That's why you should be careful in choosing your friends because the way they think is the way you're going to think. The way they speak is the way you will begin to speak. And the way they live their lives is how you will eventually live your life.

Your future is at stake, so make up your mind today to choose your friends wisely.

No Excuses

You have no excuses to be unhappy. How can I say that? Because God promises to work everything to your good—even your disadvantages and hang-ups—when you love and trust Him. After all, if you didn't have some problems, you probably wouldn't be reading this book and finding answers to your problems, would you? Even your misfortunes can work to your advantage when you have a good attitude.

Maybe your excuse is that life has been unfair to you. Well, I have to let you know the truth. Life is unfair to all of us. You can't say that you have a cross to bear, because we all have crosses to bear. Quit feeling sorry for yourself because you're disadvantaged or a certain skin color or don't have the education you need. Happiness never comes to those who feel sorry for themselves.

You know that in this world you're going to have tribulation, but you can make up your mind to be of good cheer because Jesus said He has already overcome it for you. You simply have to have faith in Him—the right attitude—to activate His saving, healing, delivering power in your life.

We have not seen, heard, or even imagined all the great things God has prepared for us. That simply means that

God has some stuff prepared for you that will simply blow your mind! Just think about that for a while and see if it is easier to have a good attitude.

There is a great story about a mule that was dumped into a deep well and left to die. Periodically dirt would get dumped into the hole, which most would see as a sign that they would soon be buried alive. Most of us would choose to sit down and die, but the mule chose a different attitude. He used every pile of dirt to step one bit closer to the top of that hole! In the end, the dirt his enemies sent to bury him provided his deliverance.

The mule had the right attitude. He rose higher and higher until he walked out of the well, and that's what God wants you to do today. Although life has thrown you in a pit and dumped on you, He wants you to get on top of the dirt and climb higher and higher. He wants you to believe that with His help you can walk out of that rut, out of that pit, out of that mess you're in. That is the right attitude—the no excuses attitude—that will make you happy and keep you happy!

Happiness matters.

"Good morning, Jesus!"

You may not feel like it, especially if you "woke up on the wrong side of the bed," but every morning you've got to get up and make up your mind to have a good attitude. You've got to say, "Good morning, Jesus! Thank You for loving me, saving me, and giving me the grace to be more than a conqueror throughout this day. No matter what I face, I know You will be with me to see me through it." Saying what you believe first thing in the morning establishes a good attitude for your day.

The difficulties in our lives and our spiritual enemies are not what defeat us. What defeats us are wrong attitudes chosen day after day concerning the issues of our lives. We will never be defeated as long as we choose to have a good attitude and trust God every day.

First thing in the morning, focus on God and His promises to you. Believe He's going to turn for your good anything the enemy throws at you. Believe that even if you mess up, He will make it right. The facts may say that you're broke, busted, and disgusted; but your attitude of faith says that as you obey God and put Him first, His blessings will overtake you in due season.

If you tend to be negative and pessimistic, it's probably a result of your upbringing and past experiences. If you have been beaten down, told you were no good, and were never encouraged; you tend to see the negative side of things. But Jesus Christ changes all that. With Jesus you do not have to be negative or pessimistic any more.

Instead of saying, "I'm a loser and I'll never change," you will say, "I'm not a loser, and I'm becoming more and more like Him." Instead of crying, "I'm afraid of everything," you will declare, "My God has not given me a spirit of fear but of power and love and a sound mind."

Every single day we have to make adjustments to keep our attitudes on track. It's not easy to keep a right attitude when we're surrounded by negative people, we live in a negative world, and everything around us is trying to steal our faith. It takes consistency and perseverance. Every day we must choose—sometimes many times a day—to have a good attitude. But it is worth the fight! A good attitude will not only bring happiness, but it will also bring success in every area of our lives.

Make up your mind to be happy by having a great attitude today! Happiness Matters. For further help contact us at, www.HeritageChristianCenter.com.

Thought 5

EIGHT POSITIVE ATTITUDES

Human beings, by changing the inner attitudes of their minds, can change the outer aspects of their lives.

William James

Did you know that Jesus told us what our inner attitudes should be and called them the be-attitudes? Of course, Jesus gave us these attitudes because He knew that if we walked in them, our lives would be dramatically changed for good and happiness would flow in our lives.

Most people believe that if they have enough money and possessions, are married to a certain kind of person, and work in the profession of their choice, then they will be happy. They soon find out that it isn't so! More money, more things, and more people in our lives only bring more responsibility, more pressure, and more stress.

What makes a human being happy is the attitude of their soul, what comes out of their inner man. And an attitude is something you put on in your heart, like the garment of praise. It is something you choose to be no matter how you feel or what is going on in your life. Following are eight beatitudes that Jesus told us to put on. Blessed actually translates as happy.

1. Blessed or happy are the poor in spirit, for theirs is the kingdom of heaven.

In this first beatitude, Jesus says that you will be happy when you are "poor in spirit." Poor in spirit means that you realize you are spiritually dead and cannot give yourself what you need—the life of God. You could reword it this way: Happy are humble people, because they realize they can't save themselves or make it on their own.

Peter tells us that God resists the proud but gives grace to the humble—those who admit they don't know everything, need God's help, and need the help of other people. God gives grace, undeserved favor, to those who are humble and submissive to His will, His Word, and His Spirit.

Proud, arrogant people think they can do anything and don't need anybody, including God. They believe that even if they fall down, they can pick themselves up and keep going. This beatitude could be worded: Cursed are the proud for they will never know God, have spiritual life, or good friends. No matter how strong you think you are, you cannot get to heaven without Jesus Christ and you cannot get through life without other people.

Our pride hates to admit that we have any weaknesses or problems that we can't handle ourselves. We are afraid that we will look bad or people will reject us. But if we will swallow our pride and humble ourselves, God will raise us up to be seated with Him in heaven and give us friends to help us on earth. Happy are you when you have the attitude that you need God and you need His people.

2. Blessed or happy are those who mourn, for they shall be comforted.

Anytime you have a loss, you will grieve; but if you admitted you were poor in spirit and needed the Lord, you have Him to comfort you. In fact, He sent the Holy Spirit to live inside you and called Him the Comforter. He is the crutch you lean on and the shoulder you cry on when life tries to crush you with tragedy and heartache.

People ask, "Why do bad things happen to good people?" I tell them that bad things happen to *all* people because sin brought us under a curse. That means people are going to do bad things to other people, and the earth is going to groan and shift under the weight of the sin of human beings. That's why we have natural disasters and crime. When you get to heaven, things will be perfect and good. But in the meantime, bad stuff is going to happen.

The Good News is that Jesus came to redeem you from the curse. When you admitted you were poor in spirit, He gave you a new spirit filled with His Spirit and set you on a course for success in every area of your life. Now, when tragedy and heartache strike you, you have the Comforter to heal you and ease your pain. All you have to do is lean on Him.

If you keep an attitude that your lifeline is Jesus Christ, then you will be comforted in a supernatural way. I have known believers who lost loved ones and unbelievers who have also lost loved ones, and the difference is staggering. Believers have the Comforter and the eternal hope of seeing their family members again that loved the Lord. They grieve in peace and with hope. But unbelievers often never stop grieving. It is like they fall into a bottomless pit of despair. And this is the case with every kind of loss. If someone betrays them, they cannot forgive them or forget the offense, and it torments them continually. They have no Comforter to give them comfort.

If you are going through a lot of pain in your life, God is not your problem. You are dealing with spiritual powers that are out to destroy you, a fallen world that is programmed by the enemy to annihilate you, and human selfishness that causes even your closest loved ones to come against you. God is not the cause of your problems; He is the solution.

If you have suffered any kind of loss, lean on your Comforter. Let Him bear your sorrow and heal your pain. After awhile you will be able to fully enjoy life again. Happy are you when you have the attitude that whenever life throws you a curve or heartache comes, you can receive comfort from the Comforter.

If you have suffered any kind of loss, lean on your Comforter.

Happiness matters.

3. Blessed or happy are the meek, for they shall inherit the earth.

Most people think that meek people are weak people, who let others walk all over them like a doormat. But the word meek actually indicates someone who has "an inward grace of the soul, calmness toward God in particular.

Meek translates today as those who are emotionally stable, kindhearted, and strong. You could reword this to say: Happy are those who know who they are in Christ, for they shall take their Promised Land. You can tell them that they are no good, they are not going to make it, and that all facts and circumstances are against them; but they will look at you and say, "I know in Whom I have believed, and I am persuaded that He will keep me and all that concerns me until the end."

The meek believer is fully calm inside because the Spirit of God controls their life. They are not a robot or a computer that God boots up every morning and makes them do everything He wants them to do. They have His peace that even when things go wrong or not as they expected, God will work it all for their good.

A meek person is not the one who flies off the handle in a rage or is abusive. Meekness is the kind of strength Jesus exhibited when he threw the moneychangers out of the temple. He did not harm anyone, but He made it known that God's house was a house of prayer. The meek are strong enough and secure enough in God to be uncompromisingly righteous yet humble and loving at the same time. They walk in such intimacy with the Holy Spirit and God's Word that their emotions stay under God's control.

Another word for the meek would be disciplined. They are spiritually disciplined to keep their carnal desires, thoughts, and emotions in check—and thus to keep their mouths shut when it is appropriate. Their faith is not in their own understanding but in God's, so their faith is strong. That's why they inherit the earth.

Happy are the emotionally stable who trust in the Lord, for they keep their eyes on the prize and never quit. They keep their focus on God's vision for their lives and do not let life steal their dreams. The attitude of the meek is that God is in control and no matter what happens He will see them through it, make them stronger, increase their faith, and prosper them in every area of their lives. The meek have a win-win attitude that always brings happiness. Happiness matters.

Be meek like Jesus. Happy are you who have the attitude that God works all things for your good, for you will take your Promised Land.

4. Blessed or happy are those who hunger and thirst for righteousness, for they shall be filled.

Righteousness is simply being right with God. You were filled with God's righteousness when you received Jesus as your Lord and Savior. Now you are right with Him, and that alone brings happiness.

The flesh will try to relieve our restlessness and dissatisfaction with things, substances, or ungodly relationships. But the only thing that will satisfy us and give us rest is seeking God and receiving more of Him and His righteousness.

Happy are you who have the attitude that you just want to be like Jesus, because you will be filled with His grace and power.

There is a law in the universe that says, whatever you sow, you will reap.

5. Blessed or happy are the merciful, for they shall obtain mercy.

There is a law in the universe that says, whatever you sow, you will reap. Whatever you give out is what you will get back. If you don't understand this principle you will live a miserable life because living is all about giving and receiving. If you don't sow love, mercy, and forgiveness, no one is going to love you, have mercy on you when you do something stupid, and forgive you when you really miss the mark.

One of the secrets to living a happy life is treating others the way you want them to treat you, and mercy is something every human being needs. We all make mistakes and mess up from time to time, and you need the mercy and understanding of God and the people who are affected by your blunders. That is why, whether someone offends you just a little or hurts you very deeply, you must show mercy. If you are critical and condemning, when you offend or hurt someone else you will be critically judged and condemned also.

If you are not happy because people are judging you and rejecting you for your mistakes, it is probably because the seed you have been sowing is the wrong kind of seed. Happy are you when you have the attitude of mercy, for then other people will treat you with mercy.

6. Blessed or happy are the pure in heart, for they shall see God.

This is an attitude of having proper motives. God is looking for those who will be honest with Him, with themselves, and with others. He knows you are a work in progress, that you are being transformed into the image of Jesus and making lots of mistakes along the way. But when you keep your heart right toward Him, He can bless you no matter how big a mess you get yourself into.

If you are single and are attracted to someone of the opposite sex, pray and ask God about it before you jump in and try to get a date. Let God direct your steps because this may not be the one He has for you—and if it is the one He has for you, you don't want to mess it up!

Trust God for everything and don't lie, control, manipulate, or dominate to try to get your way. Don't pretend you are something you're not. You are a child of God and that is your value and worth. Be who He created you to be and do what He created you to do—for Him.

Jesus didn't have any selfish motives. He was not jealous or greedy. He didn't lie to anyone or walk over them to achieve His personal agenda. His motives were pure because His heart was right toward God. His attitude was to weigh every thought, word and deed by the standard of God's Word at all times and in all situations.

If your motives are selfish and self-centered, you will not see God. That's why your life in Christ must be all about Him, not you. Happy are you who have a heart for God, for you shall see Him and know Him.

7. Blessed or happy *are* the peacemakers, for they shall be called sons of God.

Every believer is called to be a peacemaker. First of all, you have the ministry of reconciliation, which is to tell other people that they can have peace with God through Jesus Christ. Spreading the gospel is your primary responsibility as a child of God. Happy are those who bring the Good News of salvation in Jesus Christ, for they will be called the sons of God.

Secondly, you will not be recognized as a child of God on this planet if strife and division follow you everywhere you go. You are called to reconcile people to God, which brings peace into a human being's heart. Then you are called to bring peace between human beings. Jesus said, "If you are praying and remember that someone has something against you, go and be reconciled to them."

A mother who resolves a conflict between her two children is a peacemaker. Anytime you can be of assistance to resolve an issue between two people that can't agree, you are a peacemaker and God says you are His child. When you are at work and there is a dispute, don't feed the controversy. Instead, be a peacemaker. You have the Prince of Peace living inside you, and He will show you how to make peace.

Sometimes folk just want to hold on to their anger, fear, or frustration. You can pray and follow the Word and the Spirit in the situation, and move on when God tells you that your part is finished. Whether you have made peace or not is not the issue. The point is that you have done the work of a peacemaker. You have obeyed the Lord.

Happy are you who have the attitude that you will do all you know to do to make peace between people and God and to make peace between human beings, for you shall be recognized by God and other people as His mature son or daughter.

8. Blessed or happy are those who are persecuted for righteousness' sake, for theirs is the kingdom of heaven. Blessed are you when they revile and persecute you, and say all kinds of evil against you falsely for My sake. Rejoice and

be exceedingly glad, for great *is* your reward in heaven, for so they persecuted the prophets who were before you.

Jesus said a lot more about this last beatitude, probably because it deals with one of the most challenging issues a Christian will face: persecution for the gospel's sake. Anytime you sell out to the Lord, people will look at you funny. Sometimes even other believers will shun you or think you are strange when you are on fire for God.

Jesus said to rejoice in all this because you are having the same kind of impact that the Old Testament prophets had, and you will receive a great reward in heaven because of your tenacious love for God and for all the people He is drawing to Himself through your life.

Sometimes you have to say, "Mama, I love you but I have to go where God leads me. I have to go to the church He's called me to." Maybe folk are plotting against you and gossiping about you at work. Peer pressure and the desire to be liked will try to get you to back down. But if you are being persecuted, you must be on the right track!

Happy are you who have an uncompromising attitude regarding the gospel of Jesus Christ, the Word of God, and the leading of the Holy Spirit, for you will have a great reward in heaven!

For more information contact us at:
www.HeritageChristianCenter.com.

Thought 6

OPEN DOORS TO HAPPINESS

When one door of happiness closes, another opens; but often we look so long at the closed door that we do not see the one which has opened for us.

Helen Keller

Helen Keller was an amazing woman. To me, she is the perfect example of someone who had every reason to be depressed her entire life. She got sick as a baby and from that time on she could not see or hear. Yet she lived a full and a happy life and accomplished many things.

Somewhere in her life, she must have learned to turn away from the closed doors and look for the open ones. She must have understood that her faith in what could be was greater than her fear of what couldn't be. She must have conquered depression. How do I know this? Every human being deals with depression in his or her lives.

Facts About Depression

The dictionary describes depression as "low spirits; gloominess; dejection; sadness...a decrease in functional activity...characterized by feelings of hopelessness, inadequacy."[1] Isn't it interesting that the first description of depression is "low spirits." A person who is depressed has reached a point where their mind and emotions are filled with such negativity and hopelessness that their spirit becomes depressed. They feel like the weight of the world is on their shoulders and it is just too much for them to bear. They have lost so much and failed so many times that their life has become worthless.

Depression is a state of sadness, a spiritual heaviness that overtakes you. It's a heavy cloud of darkness that overshadows your thoughts and feelings. You feel and believe you are totally inadequate to meet the demands of life and can hardly function in the simplest of daily tasks. It is all you can do to get up and brush your teeth in the morning because you have either lost the meaning and purpose of your life or believe it is impossible for you to achieve it.

You will know that you're in some kind of depression when thoughts of dying occur to you. It doesn't mean that you want to kill yourself, but on the inside you really wish you could just die because life has become too overwhelming.

I've been there in my life, and I can tell you that depression will steal every bit of happiness if you let it. When I was dealing with depression, I learned some things about it. The medical journals tell us that America's number one health problem is depression. People over sixty-five are twice as likely to suffer from it. And twice as many women than men are treated for depression. People with money are three times more likely to commit suicide than people who are broke. You'd think it would be the other way around, wouldn't you? The bottom line is that money cannot give you happiness.

The second leading cause of death among college students is suicide. Obviously education cannot fill the emptiness on the inside of us any more than money can. People from all walks of life suffer from depression, even people we consider great. Abraham Lincoln and Winston Churchill both suffered from severe depression. Today it is said that one in twenty Americans is suffering from it.

Somewhere along the line, many of us—including myself—have gotten depressed. Obviously, the enemy doesn't stop trying to get us depressed just because we are a believer in Jesus Christ. It is still something we have to contend with because depression will steal your entire life if you let it. Happiness matters.

Recognizing Depression

You need to understand that depression is your enemy. Some people have become too comfortable with their "down days" and just accept them as a part of life. But you have an enemy who will increase those down days to months and years if you let him. Depression is deadly and must be stopped. You need to know that it will steal your purpose, your joy, and your future if it hangs around long enough.

You need to understand that depression is your enemy.

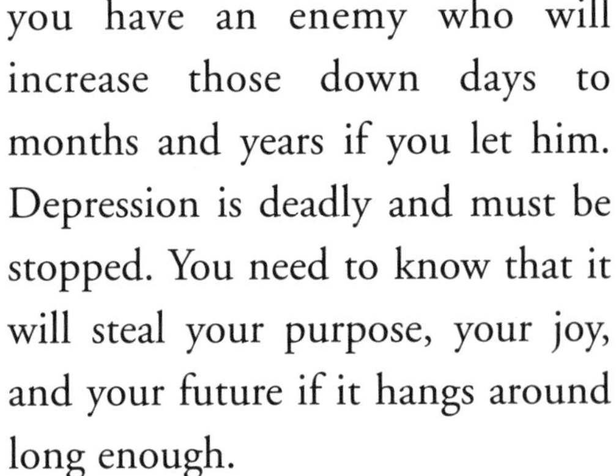

Suffering from depression is not something you need to be ashamed of either, especially since everyone you know is probably dealing with it on some level! It's something that you need to admit so you can get free of it and stay free of it. You cannot get the cure if you don't diagnose the disease. Once you know what your problem is, you can pray in and make changes in your life to overcome it.

Here are some questions that will help you identify depression.

- Are you always questioning the meaning of your life?
- Do you wonder why you were even born?
- Do you have thoughts of dying and life being over?

- Are you completely worn out mentally, physically, and emotionally?
- Have you lost all hope?
- Does your heart feel dead?
- Do you hate who you are and what you are doing?
- Does everything in your life seem worthless?
- When you look around you, do you see only a terrible, terrifying world?
- Do you feel deeply sad most of the time?

If you answered yes to any of these questions, you are probably dealing with depression. Depression will cause you to see life through a dark, negative filter. Even when something good happens to you, you cannot see it and experience it fully. The natural mind always tends to see the negative side of things, and that is where you are stuck when you are depressed.

Many situations in life can get you discouraged and depressed. You don't like being single, and you are disappointed that after so many relationships you still have not met your mate. So you lose hope, throw in the towel, and get depressed. Maybe you found out that your best friend was gossiping about you behind your back, and now everyone thinks the worst about you. You don't want to show your face at work, and you have no one to talk to about it. You feel completely alone and isolated.

Maybe the doctor has given you a bad report, and you have a tremendous battle ahead of you to get well. Could it be you are financially devastated? You have tried and tried to make ends meet but they never do. You are overworked, underpaid, and it is just too much to deal with anymore.

Some of us have to deal with the pain of an abusive past that keeps us from fully enjoying the present and paints a very dark and uncertain future. Many of us have been or are going through a divorce, which is painful and leaves us feeling like failures and losers. And the worst depression can come when our kids get into life-threatening situations like crime, drug abuse, or sexual promiscuity. We blame ourselves and feel totally helpless because nothing we do motivates them to stop.

Life can be disappointing and devastating at times. It involves tragedies, hardships, trials, tribulations, and failures. It is often difficult and demanding. And any time we experience a disappointment or a crisis, discouragement will pave the way for depression to come into our lives.

Many great men and women of the Bible became depressed and had to fight the good fight of faith to overcome it. The most famous example is Job. He had everything a man could want and lost it all. He got so depressed that he wished he had died when he was born! In the end, he got with God, repented of ever doubting His goodness and greatness, and was blessed with twice as much as he had before.

Some believers in the Bible stopped fighting the good fight of faith just after great victories. Twice Jonah said, "It is better for me to die than to live," after he had just preached to Nineveh and the whole city had repented to God! Elijah destroyed the prophets of Baal and caused it to rain after a long drought. Then, he sat down, got depressed because Jezebel was trying to kill him, and asked the Lord to die. The Lord tried to cheer him up with food and drink, asking him what was the matter. But Elijah just complained that he was the only one serving Him in all of Israel.

Both Jonah and Elijah illustrate to us that we are not just vulnerable to depression during times of tragedy or disappointment. We are also vulnerable after a great victory. We expect our lives to be a certain way after we achieve something or finally see the manifestation of a promise. When things aren't the way we thought they would be, we get depressed.

Paul was depressed because of all the persecution in his life. He asked God to take away the "thorn in the flesh" that was making his life miserable. That's when God gave him—and all believers—the answer to depression. God said, "My grace is sufficient for you, for My strength is made perfect in weakness."

David understood the principle of grace, which is exchanging our weakness for God's strength. Verse after verse in the Psalms he wrote of being in terrible crisis and torment. Then suddenly he began to praise and thank God for His saving, healing, and delivering power. After spending a number of verses extolling the virtues of God, David's whole perspective changed from hopelessness to faith to victory. When he stopped focusing on his problems and started focusing on the Lord, his entire mood and countenance changed.

No matter what your circumstances may say, no matter what the doctors or lawyers say, everything is subject to change when you're serving the Lord Jesus Christ, and His grace is sufficient for you. When you give Him your weakness, He will give you His strength to overcome. If He can go into the grave and come out of the grave, then He can help you through depression and bring you through your situation! He can restore your happiness. But you must continue to fight the good fight of faith by trusting Him over anything you feel.

Fight the Good Fight of Faith!

There are some fights that are not good. Everyone gets hurt and no one is better for them. But the fight of faith that Paul talks about is always good for you and everyone around you. It is a good fight because your faith brings God's goodness on the scene to restore everything that has been taken from you: not just your stuff, but also your joy, your peace, and your happiness. He did it for Job and He'll do it for you.

The first thing you need to know about fighting the good fight of faith is never give up! This is one of the most important keys of fighting in faith. The Bible says that if you do not faint, at just the right time you will see the manifestation of God's promise to you. Life will try to wear you down, but if you just keep going in faith you will leave depression in the dust.

> *The first thing you need to know about fighting the good fight of faith is never give up!*

Next, you need to know that our Father in heaven is in the business of restoring us—not destroying us—and there isn't anything that He cannot handle. Your mind will tell you that your problems are too great, there is no way out, and nothing will ever change. But our God is greater than any disappointment or loss, He always has a way of escape from trouble and crisis, and His miracle-working power can change any situation for our good. That includes depression.

You need to know that the root cause of depression is fear, which is the opposite of faith in God. Fear says that nothing is ever going to work out for you or be right with you, and once you believe that lie, depression has an entrance to your life. Do not budge from the truth that God is greater than anything you are facing and will work all things for your good.

God told us to be strong and courageous, to never give place to fear, and that we do that by meditating in His Word day and night. The Bible says that you are and become how you think in your heart. In other words, depression has to do with the way you are thinking. Depression thinks that all is lost. But depression lies! God's Word says all things are possible to those who believe in God.

Stop thinking about all the bad things in your life and start thinking only about the good things. Paul says that if you do this, the God of peace will be with you. Depression cannot occupy the same space as the God of all peace!

To defeat depression, you must read the Word, meditate in the Word day and night, speak the Word at all times, and pray the Word over all that concerns you. Reject every thought that opposes the Word, call it a lie, and declare the truth of God's Word instead. Make sure your thoughts and words are aligned with God's Word at all times and in all situations. Do not budge from the truth! If you go by the facts that you see today, you are going to be discouraged. But when you have faith in the truth of God's Word, the truth will overcome or change the facts.

God didn't say that weapons would stop coming against you when you gave your life to Him. He said that no weapon formed against you would succeed. Medical journals say that America's number one health problem is depression, that it is one of man's biggest emotional problems right now. But God says that the weapon of depression cannot succeed! Happiness matters.

When you fight the good fight of faith against depression, there are things you must do.

1. Eat, sleep, think, speak, and breathe God's Word.
2. Worship God with a heart of thanksgiving. Put on praise music and sing to Him until your heart gets glad.
3. Stay in church. You always need the fellowship of other believers. God did not create you to be alone, and you have a vital role to play in the body of Christ.
4. Forgive anyone who hurts you and resolve conflicts as soon as possible. Stay free of the torment of unforgiveness.
5. Take God and His Word very seriously, not yourself. Learn to laugh at yourself and especially at the lies of the enemy.

6. Have something to look forward to at the end of each day, whether it's seeing your spouse and children or walking the dog.
7. Don't let anything steal the hallelujah out of your mouth! Always see the good and praise God for it.

Depression is serious business. It will get you fired from your job, cause the breakup of your marriage, and drive your kids into sin. I don't know one depressed person who is fun to be around! If you are depressed, do these seven things and get the help you need from counselors and medical professionals. Don't let depression steal the wonderful, happy life that God has for you. Happiness matters. If you need further encouragement contact us at, **www.HeritageChristianCenter.com**.

Thought 7

PEOPLE WHO LIVE IN GLASS HOUSES...

Judge thyself with the judgment of sincerity, and thou will judge others with the judgment of charity.

John Mitchell Mason

"People who live in glass houses should not throw stones." This maxim is based on the law of sowing and reaping, that what you do to others, they will do to you. If you throw stones at others, they will throw stones at you. Jesus said, "Judge not, that you be not judged. For with what judgment you judge, you will be judged; and with the same measure you use, it will be measured back to you."

We all live in glass houses, which means we have all sinned and fall short of the glory of God. Therefore, when we see someone else sin or become overtaken with their faults and weaknesses, we have no right to judge them, to throw stones. And if we do throw stones at them, we will reap what we sowed. Someone will throw stones at us, and our glass house will shatter into a million pieces. You cannot truly be happy if you are judgmental. Happiness matters.

Are You Talking to Me?

I'm going to ask you today, "Do you take this old saying seriously?" Because I can tell you that if you don't take it seriously today, you will tomorrow. How do I know that? One day your glass house will come crashing down around you because you have been so judgmental and critical in your life. You will judge others, and your judging will come back on you.

The Bible tells us not to be judgmental. Jesus says, "Don't judge the splinter that you see in your brother's eye when you've got a log sticking out of your eye." The bottom line is that no matter who we are, we are not qualified to sit in judgment of anybody else. Jesus said that unless you pull the log out of your own eye and walk in someone else's shoes, you can't help them remove the splinter in their eye.

When you see something terrible going on in someone's life, you've got to stop and ask yourself, "Is God talking to me?" Ask yourself, "Wait a minute. Am I seeing this sin in their lives because it is in my own life? Lord, are you telling me that I need to change some things?" If you're going to be happy, you've got to get into the habit of looking at yourself with brutal honesty in the mirror of God's Word instead of rose-colored glasses.

Don't Live in a Glass House!

Pride is a glass house because it is a deception. It tells you that it is strong and will protect you, but it is glass. It will shatter at the slightest tremor of the earth or contrary wind in the air. That is why the Bible tells us that pride always brings destruction and death into our lives. Another interesting thing about glass houses is that you can see right through them. When someone who is proud, self-righteous, and arrogant walks into a room, you can see right through them. They think they are all that, that they've got it all together, but they are acting like a fool!

On the other hand, when someone who is humble and meek walks into the room, you can't see right through them because they are covered with a spiritual cloak of love and humility. Their house is made of solid rock, the Word of God. Instinctively you know that no earthquake can shake them and no hurricane can bring their house down.

You will never be happy living in a glass house. You will think you are happy, because pride and self-righteousness are deceptive. But true happiness can only come by living in the rock-solid house of God's Word, His love, and humility.

Happiness matters.

Put the Stones Down

Since whatever you throw at someone else will come right back at you, it is common sense that you will live a happier life if you just stop throwing stones. In case you didn't know by now, stones are judgmental words. The next time you see your friend Tamika with that married man, just keep your mouth shut. Don't call your friend Yolanda and have a "prayer meeting." Instead of judging her, pray for her. Instead of throwing stones, cover her with your love and prayers.

Believe it or not, God doesn't want us involved in everything we see and hear. Unless the Holy Spirit or the Word of God specifically commands us to say or do something, we need to keep our big noses out of other people's business and just pray, "God, I don't understand what's going on there, but I put it in Your hands." Then let it go and get back to your biggest challenge in life—keeping yourself right with God!

"Dennis, I am not judging them. I am just stating my own opinion. Aren't I entitled to my own opinion?" No. Not if you're judgmental, critical, and condemning. Not if you're gossiping because you think you are better than they are.

We gossip and backbite and slander other people because it makes us feel better about ourselves. Deep down we know we have a lot of problems, but pride and self-righteousness rise up when we're feeling defensive and insecure and tell us that we are better than someone else. Remember, pride and self-righteousness constitute a glass house of deception. They get you to believe you are better than anyone else.

> *The bottom line is that only Jesus has the right to judge...*

The truth, however, is that without the grace of God, there's no telling where we would all be today. If it wasn't for His mercy and the redemptive Blood of Jesus Christ, you and I could be laying under a bridge all strung out on drugs.

Maybe you haven't done some of the things other people have done, but you've thought about it. Maybe you even wanted to do it. And Jesus said that if you meditated on it in your heart, in God's eyes you are guilty of it. If you lust after another man's wife or another woman's husband, if you think about it long and hard or fantasize about it, then you are guilty of adultery.

The bottom line is that only Jesus has the right to judge because He paid the price for sin with His sinless Blood. You dethrone Jesus and sit in the King's place when you judge another human being. That's why you can't walk in His blessings if you are judgmental. So put down those stones!

The Mission of the Church

The mission of the Church is a two-edged sword. Jesus gave us the Great Commission, to go into the whole world and preach the gospel, making disciples of all nations.

We forget to love one another as Jesus loves them. The church is supposed to be a place of love and acceptance, where those who have blown it and failed and have been crushed by life can come and get healed and restored. Church may be the only place they have ever felt loved and accepted.

I'm not saying I approve of sin. I don't condone your sin because I know that your sin will eventually destroy you. But I don't have to get down on you because of what you've done. My mission is to pray for you and help you to be delivered and restored—because next week I may need your help in getting delivered from a fault and being restored!

There's a sign in front of our church building that says, "Sinners Welcome Here." We are not condoning sin, but we are saying we love you despite your sin. We are saying, "Please come and let us love you and help you to find Jesus. Then He will clean you up and get you on the right track to a happy life."

Whenever you are tempted to judge someone else, just remember where you were when Jesus came into your life. How did you see yourself? How did you treat other people? Where did you hang out and who did you hang out with? What did you talk about? When we remember the pigpen God delivered us from, we won't pick up a stone to throw. Instead we will extend the same grace and mercy to others that Jesus extended to us.

Religion Is Mean

Religious folks hung around a woman's house all night just to catch her in the act of adultery. Then they dragged her to Jesus to see what He would do. Religious people never understand Jesus because He operates by love and they operate by self-righteousness and pride.

The religious people didn't care about the woman and they don't care about you. They use the Word of God to beat you and crucify you because they have never figured out that their righteousness is filthy rags and only the Blood of Jesus saves. They still think they are better than anyone else and worthy of heaven because they tithe, work in the clothing ministry, or sing on the worship team.

Jesus confounded the religious Jews with His love and wisdom because He did things like heal people on the

Sabbath and have dinner with tax collectors. In their self-righteous eyes, Jesus was breaking the law. They could not see the higher law of love Jesus embodied. So they set a trap. They brought the woman caught in adultery to Him for His judgment. They knew they had Him now!

Under Old Testament law, the adulterous woman had to die. She was guilty. Witnesses had seen her commit the sin. Jesus stooped down in front of the woman and the church elders and began to write in the dirt. We don't know what He wrote, but personally I think he wrote the elders' sins in the dirt.

Then Jesus said that whoever had no sin in their lives should throw the first stone. The Bible says that one by one they put their stones down and walked away. Religion is always rendered powerless in the face of God's saving love and grace.

I don't like the way Hollywood presents Christianity, but sometimes they are correct. Christianity can become a dead religion just like the rest. When all you see are the rules and laws and dos and don'ts, and you forget the saving grace and living relationship with God through Jesus Christ, you are religious, not spiritual.

Religion is mean, harsh, and judgmental because it is based upon law and not grace. Religion will make folk as mean as a junkyard dog! Don't fall into legalistic, cold-hearted, self-righteous religion. Fall into the arms of Jesus!

Then you can look at others as He does, be compassionate instead of judgmental, and live a happy life. Happiness matters.

Love Covers

Love pierces hearts and draws people to Jesus to be set free and restored. It is the goodness of God that leads us to repentance.

It's simple. If you want to be happy don't live in a glass house! Humbly examine yourself and pray instead of throwing stones, and then go to the one who is in trouble and be the instrument of love God uses to restore them. If you live your life like this, you will live in a solid house that nothing can shake, and your own happiness will be secure in Jesus. Happiness matters. For more information contact us at www.HeritageChristianCenter.com.

Thought 8

SIMPLIFY YOUR LIFE

Slow down and enjoy life. It's not only the scenery you miss by going too fast-you also miss the sense of where you are going and why.

Eddie Cantor

My wife said to me one day, "Why are you going so fast?"

I said, "I don't know."

It was then I realized that we are always in a hurry. We dodge in and out of traffic like we are crazy, racing from one stoplight to the next. We gun it when the light turns green, then slam on the brakes when the next light turns red.

I asked myself the question, "What is so important?" We are all rushing around as though our lives depended on it. In reality, they don't! But the only way we are going to see what's really important is to stop and simplify our lives.

The Fast Pace of Life

When we get caught up in a fast pace of life, we become aggressive, demanding, and just plain rude. Today women pursue men with as much aggression as men pursue women. If a clerk in a store doesn't have what we want, we will tell them off. And when traffic stops, we now have a thing called "road rage."

If something does not happen as we planned, the nearest person available gets hammered. People have high expectations; and when those expectations are not met, they have no patience for the shortcomings of others and zero tolerance for their inability to meet their need.

When we run in fifth gear with pressure, stress, and frustration on our heels, we usually forget the smallest kindness or courtesy. Our excuse is that we don't have time and are too worn out. We don't know our neighbors' names and are too tired to care. We go home, hit the garage door opener, drive in, close the door, and shut the world out.

I was walking the dogs one morning and a lady who lives about four doors down came out. She said, "I thought I'd introduce myself to you since you've been in the neighborhood about two and half years." I thought of the old days. When someone moved into the neighborhood, everyone would go over and introduce themselves. Today we don't even think about it.

Our generation is not only thoughtless but also restless. We are more self-centered and driven by success, money, and keeping up with the Joneses. Modern technology tells us that it is saving us so much time and energy, yet we are tied to the bizarre rhythm of it, constantly pushing buttons and communicating with everyone we know by cell phone, computers, and the Internet.

All of this makes us oversensitive, and we often overreact. We are easily upset by our jobs, family members, relationships—even God. We get frustrated when He doesn't move fast enough or do what we want Him to do. Everyday occurrences get on our last nerve and send us into a tailspin. The check-out line at the grocery store. Getting a decent parking place. And although we are always rushing, we're always late.

How can we be happy living like this? We have to simplify our lives if we are going to be happy. Happiness matters.

First Things First

A few years ago God said to me, "Dennis, you've got to stop and smell the roses. Life is like a vapor. It's here one minute and it's gone the next."

I knew He was right. I was a pusher, and when God gave me a promise I wanted it to happen today. Consequently, I drove myself and everyone around me to get it done in a day. But over time I realized that I could not be happy and be a workaholic. I could get a lot of work done, but I would sacrifice my happiness and eventually my health.

One of the first things that I needed to get straight was my priorities. I knew God was first, but I had to revisit that truth and make certain I was incorporating it into my daily life. I knew that the key to everything else was maintaining a close, right relationship with Him.

What's Hot and What's Not

There used to be a time when we could entertain ourselves with the smallest and most unusual things. When I was a kid, we would take an old lawnmower, pull the wheels off of it, and put it on a piece of plywood to make it into a go-cart. We could play with a stick and a can and be happy. But today our kids have got to have high tech games and toys, the best equipment, and $150 shoes to play a sport.

We seem to be obsessed with living the good life, but we can't enjoy the life that we have. The grass is always greener on the other side. We think we will be happy and content if we have more money, get that promotion, and marry a certain kind of person. But even if we attain these things, we never seem to be satisfied.

Wall Street and the advertising firms have got us wrapped up in what's hot and what's not. They are not just peddling materials things, either. They are selling a whole way of life. They tell us we won't be happy unless we live in a certain house, work in a certain profession, drive a certain car, wear certain clothes, and possess certain electronic equipment. They tell us what movies and television programs to watch, where to spend our vacation, what to eat and drink, and where get the best deals in town.

If you are going to simplify your life, you are going to have to set some boundaries.

The world pressures us to know everything they think we need to know, possess all the things they believe we need to possess, and experience all they think we need to experience. It's like a three-ring circus! If we don't do it their way, we are missing it. We are told again and again that their road is the road to happiness—and guess what? God is not on it.

Let me tell you something the advertising executives and Wall Street will not tell you. The more successful you are and the more stuff you own, the more stress and pressure you have. More stuff equals more responsibility, requires more of your time, and the enemy has more opportunities to drive you, ride you, and run you into the ground.

If you are going to simplify your life, you are going to have to set some boundaries. You need to spend time with your spouse and your children, taking an active interest in their lives. You cannot take on too much work, but you must do excellent work and show integrity in the workplace.

Financial Stewardship — Oh My!

Money. We all have to have it, but it is one of the greatest causes of stress and problems in our lives. If you are going to simplify your life and be happy, you have to deal with the money issue head-on. If you are under financial pressure because you are living above your means, you need to downsize, set a budget, and get out of debt. You've got to cut up your credit cards if you're under excessive debt and start spending only what you have to spend. The only way to use a credit card is to pay it off every month, and you have to submit to a budget and have the self-discipline to do that.

We are told to lay aside every weight and sin that sets you back and entangles you so that you can win your race. In your finances, that means you've got to sit down and figure out what's going on! Write down how much money comes in and how much money goes out each month. If more money is going out than is coming in, you must downsize. Pray and ask God what to cut, and if you need help from a financial counselor, don't hesitate to see them. Getting your finances straight is vital to your happiness and happiness matters.

Half the battle in your finances is always knowing what is going on. It is when you don't keep track of spending and come up short that you get bent out of shape. One of the keys to financial stability is being aware at all times what you and your spouse are spending and making certain you have that money to spend.

If you are in debt, you must get out. Again, depending on how bad your situation is, you may need a financial professional to help you with a plan. And the plan you come up with may mean moving into a smaller house, not eating out as much, or selling some things. In other words, your lifestyle may change.

The problem people have is lust of the eyes. They see something, they want it, they buy it—with a credit card. Then the credit card bill comes in, and they don't have the money to pay it. So stick to your plan! Know what you have and where it must go. Don't go into debt over things you really don't need.

Besides the lust of the eyes, our families can complicate things. We want our loved ones to have the best, so we are tempted to go beyond our means. Our kids have grown and need new clothes for school. Johnny is really excited to join the junior high band and learn the guitar—the music teacher says he is a natural—so he asks you to buy one for him.

Our heavenly Father doesn't give us everything we want, and neither should you. Instead, educate your kids on being good stewards of what God has given. Involve them in the financial workings of the family. Sit down with Johnny and see what you have to work with to buy that guitar. Is there a job he could do to earn the money? What about renting one? After all, in six months he might realize that is not his calling and quit.

Too many people are in a financial mess because they spend first and count the cost later.

Too many people are in a financial mess because they spend first and count the cost later. They go to church and ask for the pastor to agree with them for a financial miracle when their real problem involves greed, selfishness, and bad stewardship.

Sometimes you just have to say no to your flesh! Greed and lust must be defeated. If you give in to them, you will only find misery. But if you become a good steward and keep your financial life in order, you will be able to tithe and give as you would like to give, pay your bills, enjoy what you have, be a powerful witness for the gospel message, and stop and smell the roses from time to time. Happiness matters.

Understanding Pressure

Even the apostle Paul said, "I feel pressed in on every side." He oversaw many churches and was continually preaching and adding churches. He had to straighten out the messes others caused. Civil authorities and enemies schemed against him, beat him, imprisoned him, or ran him out of town. Paul had a lot of pressure and stress, but it did not come from God.

There is something you need to know about casting your cares on the Lord, however. He cannot relieve the stress and pressure while you are in disobedience. One of the reasons you experience discomfort is because you are in the wrong place at the wrong time doing the wrong thing with the wrong people. Until you repent and get back in His will, He can't help you. If you climb the corporate ladder and neglect your family to do it, God cannot relieve you of the pressure and stress. His hands are tied because your priorities are out of order. And what good is it to get to the top and lose your family?

Whether you are in God's will or out of God's will, you are going to encounter stress and pressure. But if you are in God's will you can travel light! He'll carry the burdens and take the weight when you love Him and serve Him with your whole heart.

Remember, the enemy will drive you to the point where you quit. He will increase the stress until you wear out, forget priorities, and stop moving. His ultimate goal is for you to kill yourself by overwork or by taking your own life. That's why simplifying your life is so important. Happiness matters.

When you realize the pressure has gotten to you, look to Jesus and get relief. How do you spell relief? J-E-S-U-S!

The Rhythm of a Godly Life

Years ago I considered leaving the ministry. If you have enough stress in your life, you will want to run away; and I had reached that point. That's when God said, "Well Son, you don't ever take a vacation or do anything except preach and study."

I came to the conclusion that I needed to enjoy life more. We began going to Mexico once a year, and I really enjoyed it. One day I said, "Let's go twice this year." Now I try to go as often as possible. This was one of the ways I began to simplify my life, but you might find other ways to break your routine and do something different. Take the dog for a walk. Go to the gym and work out. Go to a movie. Buy somebody a present. Throw a barbecue and invite friends over.

Simplifying your life could mean taking more time off. It could mean working fewer hours and spending time with your family—or not using your family as an excuse not to work. We are all different. Our gifts and callings, personalities, and situations in life are different. But there are certain principles that hold true for everyone.

There comes a time when we have to say, "I'm tired of rushing around, stressing out, and being under pressure all the time. I'm going to slow down and get my life in order. And I'm going to let God carry my burdens and keep me on track. I don't want to waste my life."

I encourage you to walk with God and fall into His rhythm of life. The world's hectic pace will make you think you are getting somewhere when you are going nowhere. But God's rhythm is the very definition of happiness for a human being. When you get in sync with Him, you will truly enjoy your life.

Happiness matters. For more information contact at **www.HeritageChristianCenter.com.**

Thought 9

GRASSHOPPERS AND LOW SELF-ESTEEM

Human beings can only be truly happy with themselves by gazing into the mirror of the Holy Scriptures and seeing themselves as their Creator sees them.

Anonymous

Every morning and evening, at times during the day, and whenever we are getting ready to go out on a special occasion, we all look at ourselves in the mirror. What do we see? Some of us see a person we like and even love. Some of us see someone we are ashamed of, embarrassed by, and even hate. But most of us are somewhere in between, trying to accentuate the positive and minimize the negative.

The Bible says, "As a man thinks in his heart, so is he." In other words, how you see yourself is one of the things that will make the difference between you being a happy person or a miserable person. Therefore, it is vital that you see yourself correctly, and the only person who can tell you who you really are and what you are really worth is the One who created you. God is the only one who can define your life.

We can despise ourselves when we give our lives to the Lord, and all of a sudden we start liking ourselves. We look in our bathroom mirror and see ourselves in a totally different light. Instead of being miserable with ourselves, we begin to be happy with ourselves.

Happiness matters.

"We Look Like Grasshoppers"

The children of Israel came to the Promised Land. Moses sent twelve spies in to see what was there and report back to him and the people. Joshua and Caleb reported, "It is a great land, and we can take it because God said we could. He's given us favor and now is the time."

The other ten spies reported, "It's a great place, but there are also giants. Next to them we look like grasshoppers. We cannot fight these people and win." As you know, God was not pleased with the majority report, and Israel walked in the desert for forty more years. Most of them died and never saw the Promised Land.

After seeing the miraculous power of God deliver them again and again, including the parting of the Red Sea, what caused the children of Israel to doubt God's promise to them and fear the giants so much that they refused to go into the Promised Land? It is the same reason you are afraid of the enemy and cannot possess all God has given you today: low self-esteem.

By the time Moses came on the scene, they had a slavery mentality and an abusive, painful past. They had been so beaten down physically, mentally, and emotionally that they had little or no self-esteem. When they saw the giants in the Promised Land, they remembered the mighty pyramids of Egypt instead of the parting of the Red Sea. As a result, they saw themselves as grasshoppers and forgot who they were. Because they had more faith in their own weakness than they had in God's promise to them, they missed God's best.

You Are Valuable and Precious to God

Anytime someone has had an abusive past, their tendency is to have low self-esteem, and it is hard for them to even consider that they are worthy of the promises of God. When someone who has been mistreated in their past hears the Word of God, it's difficult for them to believe it. They cannot imagine that God will hear their prayers and answer them.

The enemy's goal since the Garden of Eden has been to get us to doubt God's love, Word, and faithfulness. He said to Eve, "Did God really mean what He said?" and she fell for it. Unfortunately, we are still falling for it today; and one of the ways our spiritual enemy gets us to doubt God is to have those we love and trust abuse us, then we will think we are worthless, unlovable, and a nobody. Why would God help us?

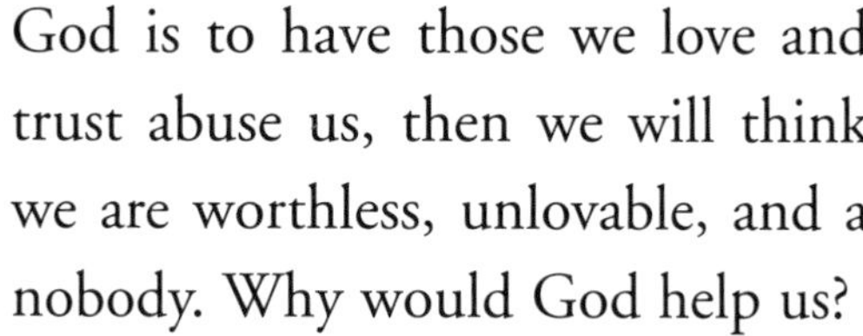

> *You are not worthless, unlovable, or a nobody to God or to God's people.*

You are not worthless, unlovable, or a nobody to God or to God's people. He loves you so much that He sent Jesus to die on the cross to pay for your sin and make a way for Him to adopt you as His child for eternity. In fact, He would have sent Jesus to die for you if you had been the only person to ever accept Jesus as Lord and Savior.

Dealing With the Enemy

Even after you have given your life to the Lord, the enemy's plan is for you to be so cast down that you think you are not worth much to anyone, but especially to God. His plan is to discourage you so you think you are not worthy of God's attention or help.

First of all, everyone is messed up. There isn't a human being on earth who hasn't been treated badly by other human beings. None of our parents are perfect, and neither are our teachers, church leaders, employers, spouses, children, and grandchildren. All of us have sinned and fall short of the glory of God.

You say, "But Dennis, you don't know how perverse my life has been. I've lived in some of the worst failures imaginable." I will tell you the truth. The apostle Paul was the worst sinner ever because he said he was. He said he was filled with so much hatred, anger, and jealousy that he killed Christians. Yet look what God did to, through, and for old Saul of Tarsus. He became the apostle Paul, who wrote much of the renewed covenant and brought the gospel to people all over the ancient world.

It's time for you to quit believing the lies of the enemy and believe God's Word instead. You are more than a conqueror through Jesus Christ who loves you. You can accomplish great things because the Greater One lives inside you. Every day you are going from faith to faith and glory to glory as you allow God's Word to transform you into the image of Christ Jesus.

The root of all self-esteem issues is the lie that God does not love you or like you, but the enemy also uses little lies to break you down. He uses culture and society to get you upset over the most trivial issues. For example, let's say you are feeling insecure and turn on the TV. The commercials and the programs tell you what the perfect body should look like. Of course, your body is not perfect, and after an hour or two you want to hide in a cave.

The truth is, you are physically healthy and attractive, but now you feel ugly and worthless. Why? You believed a couple of little lies from the enemy. That's why it is so important for you to see yourself through God's eyes and not the eyes of society or other people.

To be happy, you must refuse to believe his lies. Get rid of them by choosing to believe God's Word instead. Find verses that oppose each lie and live in the truth until it is so much a part of you that you don't even question it anymore. Don't let low self esteem beat you down anymore!

Who Are You?

Genesis 1:27 tells us that God created us in His image, and that truth alone gives us good reason to feel unique and special. If your parents never told you that, you can tell it to yourself—and your children. From a very early age, you need to say, "Baby, you are beautiful. You are God's princess. Son, you are so handsome. You're a mighty man of God."

Remember, you will become what you believe yourself to be and do only what you believe you are capable of doing. And your spiritual enemy wants you to look in the mirror and see a loser. He will tell you that you are a mistake. No one wanted you to be born. You were sexually and physically abused because you are an evil person, and you deserve to be hit. There is something really wrong with you. You just turn people off.

You must destroy this false, destructive self-image and replace it with God's truth. Find out and then stand in who you are in Christ Jesus. God doesn't make junk, and that includes you! And if no human being wanted you to be born, God did. You are the apple of His eye, and He loved you before anyone ever thought of you. As for sexual and physical abuse, you were victimized, but you are no longer a victim. You are washed clean by the Blood of the Lamb and God sees you as holy.

God doesn't make junk, and that includes you!

Proverbs 24:16 says that though a righteous man falls seven times, he will rise again. When you've got the Greater One inside you, you can rise above the problems of your past. Even if your earthly father doesn't love you, you have a heavenly Father who can fill every hole in your soul.

No matter what damage your family, friends, school, or society has done to you, if you will sell out to the Lord, He will clear away the damage of your past and give you the strength to forgive those who have hurt you. Read my chapter on forgiveness again and again because if you don't forgive you will be tormented, stuck in a rut, and forfeit what God has for you. Forgiving sets you free and allows God's blessings to flow into your life. Forgiving others allows happiness to come and happiness matters.

The Lord will also help you get past the limits you have placed on yourself. In Him you learn that all things are possible. You have authority over the enemy and will not believe his lies. In Christ you overcome your past, resist temptation to sin, and kick out the forces of darkness that have oppressed you and lied to you your entire life.

So who are you? You are a child of Almighty God. You are loved and precious in His sight. You are a vital member of the body of Christ, important to Him and to His kingdom. You are on your way to heaven to enjoy eternal bliss. You are not a grasshopper; you are somebody special! Enjoy your life because happiness matters.

Your Life Reflects Your Self-Image

I can always tell what people think of themselves by the people they associate with. When they have a grasshopper mentality they will associate with people who talk down to them and degrade them. Single people with a poor self-image tend to date those who aren't good enough for them. In fact, if they think they are nothing but a grasshopper, they will probably marry somebody who is an abusive giant.

When we have a bad self-image, we tend to think that we are not good enough to be blessed. If we haven't dealt with the issue of low self-esteem, we tend to think that we could never own our own home, run our own business, hold a good job, be a good husband and father or wife and mother, or minister to other people. Because we see ourselves as grasshoppers, we never enter our Promised Land.

If you don't have a good opinion of yourself, there is no evil that you can't fall into. You will believe you are capable of every failure imaginable.

However, with a God-given self-image and godly self-esteem, there is no limit to what you can be and accomplish. After all, you have Greatness inside you. The Holy Spirit lives in your heart! He gives you the strength to stop going to bars, sleeping with strangers, stealing from your community, and lying about all of it.

The mere fact that the Spirit of God lives inside you says that you are valuable and precious. You cannot lose with Jesus! Even if you stumble and fall or fail from time to time, He is there to help you get up, learn from it, and get going again.

When you know that God has great plans for you, it will change the way you live your life. You will walk away from your prairie chicken friends and begin to soar with the eagles! You'll stop watching certain movies and television programs. You'll take better care of your body, which is His temple, and get your priorities in order.

Who Will You Become?

There is a story that when Michelangelo bought a large piece of marble to sculpt, one of his friends asked, "Why did you buy that? It's got all kinds of flaws in it."

Michelangelo replied, "Because I see an angel locked up in that marble."

You may be flawed in your flesh, but God sees an angel locked up inside you. When the Master Sculptor begins to work with you, He's going to create something beautiful out of your life.

Have you ever been to a garage sale or an antique show? There are things that look like junk because of where they've been and how they've been treated. But to the trained eye, they are treasures ready to be found and unlocked. God is the expert with the trained eye. Even though the enemy says you are trash, God sees the treasure in you.

If you had known me and observed my life years ago you would not have thought much of me. But God saw something in me that nobody else could see. He saw potential that I had no idea was there. As He lives in me and I live in Him, His greatness is released and my life has a joy and meaning I never dreamed of.

You are unique, like a snowflake. There is nobody like you! When you look into the mirror of God's Word, you still may see someone who makes a lot of mistakes and fails from time to time. But keep reminding yourself that God sees something different. He sees what you're becoming as you put Him first in your life.

God knows and you now know that there is a lion inside you! You are a champion, a warrior, and a survivor. So it's time to quit putting yourself down. You need to say to yourself, "God loves me for who I am, and I can love myself. I am created in His image. Jesus died for me so I could be with Him forever. I was created to love and to be loved. I am the righteousness of God by the Blood of Jesus Christ. I am pure and holy and good in His sight. And I am NOT a grasshopper!" Therefore I can be happy and happiness matters. If you need assistance contact us at HeritageChristianCenter.com.

Thought 10

FEAR STEALS HAPPINESS

"The only thing we have to fear is fear itself."

Franklin D. Roosevelt

Hearts Failing for Fear

About a dozen years ago the Lord began to deal with me about all the fears in my life. I didn't think I had any! But as the Lord revealed things to me, I began to realize how many things I was afraid of. He took me back to my childhood, and I remembered having very negative feelings from the time I was a little boy. Twice I was hit by a car while riding my bicycle. It's amazing I'm still here!

After these traumatic things happened, I developed a fear that I was going to die at an early age. This was one of the fears the Lord revealed to me, and I knew it was time for me to put them to rest. Paul said that there came a time when he had to put away childish things, and that day had arrived for me. The Lord said that if I didn't deal with these fears, I would never fulfill my destiny in Him.

No matter who we are, we all have fears that we must overcome.

You are no different from me in that respect. No matter who we are, we all have fears that we must overcome. Fears may be introduced into your life as a child or come to you as an adult, but all human beings deal with fear. Jesus said that in these last days people's hearts would fail them because of fear. I have no doubt we are living the last days!

There are so many reasons and ways to be afraid. We can be afraid of dying or growing old. We can fear our loved ones dying and growing old. We can be afraid of being alone. We can fear other cultures and colors of people. The root of prejudice and racism is fear. Fear destroys courage when you become discouraged, so fear is the root cause of discouragement and depression. There is the fear of a spouse being unfaithful, our children having sex before marriage or getting into drinking and drugs, and all the things that can destroy a family.

Some people who have worked for me have not succeeded simply because they were afraid to make a mistake, so they became indecisive. They were too afraid to make decisions. Any area of timidity in your life is rooted in fear. The enemy wants you to be afraid of losing something: your health, a spouse, your finances, your reputation, someone's love, a job, even a ministry. Then he can stop you from moving forward in God.

Today we could be terrified day and night if we just gave in to every fear that comes from watching the news. There are new viruses and diseases being discovered, and many of the ones we already know about are painful or incurable or both. The economies of the world are hanging in the balance and America is not doing too much better. Our stock market goes up and down like a yo-yo, our national debt is through the roof, social security has a bleak future, and recent national disasters have spending out of control.

Then there's terrorism and Islamic jihad. The specter of September 11, 2001, is always in our minds. Nearly every day we hear a report of how many lives are lost from suicide bombers and radical insurgents throughout the Middle East, including Israel. According to Scripture, it will only get worse before Jesus comes back.

We are living in the last days, and it's no accident that terrorism has emerged as the way to try to dominate the people of the world because the chief terrorist is Satan. He has always been a terrorist, and now he is pulling out everything he's got because he knows that his time is short.

The Chief Terrorist

Satan is the ruler of the kingdom of darkness, and he rules by fear. Jesus is the king of the kingdom of God, and He rules by love. Satan pressures people to obey him with terrorist fear tactics; Jesus encourages people to obey Him because He loves them. First John 4:18 says that perfect love, or God's love, casts out all fear. Now more than ever, the two kingdoms are at war, and believers in Jesus Christ must dress for battle by building their faith in God and walking in His perfect love. Otherwise, fear will hold us captive and keep us from fulfilling the plan that God has for our life.

The enemy can control and eventually destroy your entire life if you give in to the chief terrorist? Fear is a powerful spiritual force, and the enemy's objective is to paralyze believers with fear so that he can rule the earth and keep Jesus from ruling it through us.

I have had moments in my life that I was so paralyzed by fear all I could do was shake. I thought I had lost everything, and my life would never be right again. What pulled me through was getting into God's Word and reminding myself that God had not given me a spirit of fear. He had given me a spirit with power, love, and a sound mind.

Power, Love, and a Sound Mind

You have all the ability and equipment to defeat fear in your life. Your reborn spirit contains God's power, His love, and the mind of Christ. You also have God's Word, the sword of the Spirit, which destroys the lies and attacks of the enemy that would otherwise cause fear. Thoughts of fear will come, but you don't have to sit down and entertain them.

Your adversary prowls about like a roaring lion, seeking whom he may devour, but you can resist him steadfastly in the faith. If you don't give into fear, he can't devour you. You see, he is a toothless lion! He makes a lot of noise, but in reality he is powerless in the face of a believer who knows who they are in Christ—and that Jesus has already defeated him.

The Bible says in Colossians 2:15 that Jesus disarmed all demonic principalities and powers and publicly humiliated them. They have no weapons. The only thing they can do is try to get you to accept their lies, deception, fear, anger, jealousy, and every other evil work. You must understand that they will roar and scream and do everything they can to terrify you because that's all they've got! They know that in Jesus Christ you have already defeated them.

Now I know all this, and I still get scared from time to time. But you can feel fear and not react to it. You can be so afraid on the inside you don't know if you're going to make it, but on the outside you don't let the devil see you sweat. You refuse to believe, speak, or act like you are afraid because deep inside you know you aren't. Although your flesh is afraid, your spirit is filled with power, love, and a sound mind.

Faith Defeats Fear

First John 5:4 says, "And this is the victory that has overcome the world—our faith." It didn't say, "You must have fantastic, insurmountable faith to overcome and see the victory." It said you just have to use what you've got. One of the enemy's tactics is to tell you that your situation is so impossible and so difficult that you just don't have enough faith for it.

We must walk by faith and not by sight to overcome fear.

If I had lived by my feelings I would still be in the construction business. Instead, I used the faith in God that I had. I trusted Him more than any feeling, fact, or circumstance, and as a result I have the joy and honor of helping to build spiritual houses instead of physical houses. Our church is thriving because all of our staff and our members are also using their faith in God instead of giving in to fear and intimidation.

We must walk by faith and not by sight to overcome fear. I have known people who have been saved for fifty years, but they are still baby Christians because they never learned how to walk by faith and not by sight. They are afraid of everything, and they have missed so many blessings as a result. Fear will cause you to miss God's blessings, and if you miss God's blessings you will not be happy. Happiness matters.

You Choose Faith or Fear

In every situation in your life, you will choose to either walk in faith or give in to fear. How do I know this? Because the enemy is like a roaring lion who will try to devour you with fear any time he has the opportunity. If he can stop you with fear, you will cease to be a threat to the kingdom of darkness and become unproductive in the kingdom of God. So I guarantee that he will be bombarding you with thoughts of terror every time you get up to do something for the Lord.

This may be hard to hear, but people who walk in fear usually fail. It's what we refer to as "Job's Law." Job made the statement that what he had most feared had come upon him. He was afraid of losing everything, and so he lost everything. Why does this work? Fear is having more faith in the enemy to do evil and bring destruction in your life than you have in God to do good and bring blessings in your life.

If you are afraid of getting hurt, you have faith to get hurt. Consequently, you will never have a relationship with another human being (which is a failure in itself), or you will be hurt in every relationship because you have more faith to be hurt than you do to be blessed by God or that His grace will pull you through any hurt you might encounter.

The children of Israel feared that they were grasshoppers in the sight of the giants and could never take the Promised Land from them—and they didn't! They wandered in the wilderness for forty years and never fulfilled God's will for their lives. That's why we must be like Joshua and Caleb. We must believe the Word of God, have faith in Him to perform it, and have the courage to move toward our Promised Land. We must not fear!

Paul said to give no place to the enemy. In other words, when you let fear stay in your life as a child of God, you make a place for the enemy to come in and steal your happiness, your joy, and everything else that you have in this life. You don't have to be a drug addict for the enemy to defeat you. All you've got to do is make decisions based on the fears in your life instead of your faith in God. You will either conquer fear or fear will conquer you.

Without faith it's impossible to please God. Without fear it's impossible to please the enemy. If failure keeps knocking at your door you've got to stop and say, "Wait a minute! Is fear controlling my life?" Fear will cause you to quit, to give up too soon, and to throw in the towel before you have victory. It is to render you useless to God.

Sometimes you've got to make some tough decisions to walk by faith. You know the man you're dating is abusive, and he stole money out of your purse, but you're afraid of being alone. Get rid of your fear and have faith in God to bring you a good, godly husband. Your fear of being alone is the enemy's tactic to get you to mess up God's plan for your life.

Fear causes people to do crazy things, even making them superstitious. They're afraid to break a mirror or seven years of bad luck will come upon them. They're afraid to step on a crack, walk under a ladder, or let a black cat cross in front of them. They carry a rabbit's foot or a four leaf clover in their pocket.

David said that he sought the Lord and He delivered him from all his fears. If you're walking in superstition it's because you're walking in fear. I encourage you to put an end to superstition and trust God instead.

There is only one way you can build your faith in God, and that is to spend time with Him in His Word. Faith comes by hearing and hearing by the Word of God, so you must saturate your mind and heart with Scripture. As you build your faith in God through His Word, He will also give you information you need to know to fight the enemy and win the victory.

When you go into a confrontation with the enemy armed with God's Word—the sword of the Spirit—and

His knowledge and wisdom concerning the situation you are in, then you have confidence to fight the good fight of faith and win. Because fear is built on emotions, bad news, and negative reports, you need to know what God says about your situation in order to defeat the fear.

Step Out of the Boat and Keep Your Eyes on Jesus

We all know the story of when Jesus walked on the water toward the disciples' boat during a storm. He told Peter that he could walk on the water and come to Him. In faith Peter went over the side of the ship and took a few steps on the water. But then he took his eyes off of Jesus to look at the storm, fear gripped him, and he began to sink. That's when Jesus reached out and caught him.

Anytime you step out in faith the enemy will bring a storm your way. He wants to frighten you and get your eyes off of Jesus. But even if you fall for it and start sinking, Jesus is there to pull you up and keep you going in your walk with Him. The next time the storm comes, however, keep your eyes on Jesus and refuse to give in to fear. Then watch what God will do!

God says, "Fear not," 366 times in the Bible. That's one for every day of the year and one for good measure. Say it and mean it! Don't let the storm of fear stop you from being who God created you to be and doing what He's created you to do.

Don't be the guy who buried his talent because he was afraid of his master! Get your talent out there and use it as God intended, declaring, "I do not fear because God has redeemed me. He has called me by name. I will walk through flood and fire and not be harmed because He is my strength and deliverer!"

I can be happy if I confront my fears and walk by faith and not by sight. Happiness matters. For more encouragement contact us at www.HeritageChristianCenter.com.

Thought 11

BEING A PEOPLE PERSON

There are two types of people-those who come into a room and say, "Well, here I am," and those who come into a room and say, "Ah, there you are."

Frederick Collins

One of the reasons one person is happy and another person is miserable is because the happy person is a people person and the unhappy person is not. The way this works is simple. If you relate well with people and they like you, they are going to help you and bless you. They will want you to succeed and be happy. But if you are self-centered and don't care about people, they won't care about you either.

If you have been unconcerned and uncaring about other people up until now, you have probably been unhappy. I challenge you to make some changes in the way you think, speak, and act around others because I know your life will be so much happier. The following points will help you and motivate you to become more of a people person.

1. You cannot change other people, but you can change yourself. You cannot change where you have been and what you have done, but you can change where you are going; and you do that by changing yourself, not others.

The main thing you need to ask yourself is, how do you treat others? The way you treat others is the way you will be treated. It is the law of sowing and reaping. If you don't like the way people are treating you, you've got to stop and ask yourself, "What am I sowing, because I don't like what I'm reaping?"

If you work in a store and treat your customers poorly, chances are they will not buy anything and they won't be back. If you disrespect your employer, you probably won't get a raise—and you might get fired. You get back what you give out.

Take a good look at how you think about other people, how you speak to them, and how you behave toward them. Consider their reactions to you. If you don't take off your "mask of perfection" and get honest, you will spend your life evaluating everyone else's faults and weaknesses instead of considering your own. And if you do that, you will never see where you are deficient in relating to other people.

Instead of complaining that you have such a hard time getting along with people, ask yourself, "Do people have a difficult time getting along with me?" If you don't know, just ask those who are closest to you, and they'll tell you. These are some of the statements you may have heard from time to time that can give you big clues:

"You're on a real power trip."

"You hurt my feelings when you talk to me like that."

"You have a bad attitude, and you need to go back to bed."

"You act like you don't love me at all."

"You know, you just make me feel stupid."

"I'm scared to say anything I really think or feel when I'm around you".

If people have said any of these things to you, then it means you are not treating them right. I think the two most important questions you can ask yourself right now are: How do I want to be treated? Am I treating other people that way? When you have the answers to those questions, you can begin to change.

2. Put yourself in someone else's place instead of putting them in their place. Before you give someone a piece of your mind, stop a second and imagine walking in their shoes. Instead of telling them off, try to relate to their situation and circumstances. Then you can treat them with

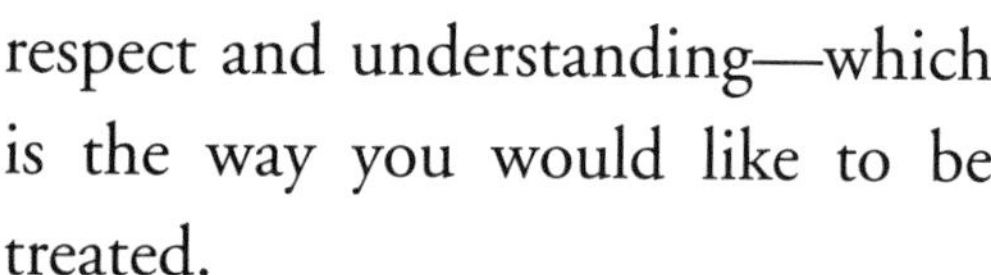

respect and understanding—which is the way you would like to be treated.

You cannot really solve a problem with another person without first seeing the situation through their eyes.

When people put you down or are critical and negative, you can't relate to them and you don't want to relate to them. In fact, when the phone rings you check the caller ID to see if it is one of them because you are sick of their negative talk.

If you don't like to be around people who are always pointing out your faults and weaknesses, neither does anyone else. That tells you that nothing gets solved by putting someone down. When you put someone in their place, you are putting them down. You are not solving any problems either.

You cannot really solve a problem with another person without first seeing the situation through their eyes. And when you see it from their perspective, sometimes you see something you didn't see before and change your mind. This is humbling, but you cannot relate to people in a right way and be arrogant. You have to stay humble and remind yourself that God loves them and Jesus died for them too.

Nordstrom's has a policy that the customer is always right, and they treat their customers the way they want to be treated. Their employees are to smile and be friendly no matter how the customer treats them. Isn't that the way we all want to be treated at all times?

The next time someone crosses you, take a deep breath and think before you speak. Consider the other person's point of view before you make a judgment. The other person will appreciate it, especially if they were misunderstood or needed a gentle and kind person to correct them.

3. Encourage and lift up people. A charismatic person always makes you feel good about who you are. That's why they are charismatic! They want to help you and bless you in any way they can.

The happiest people on earth are those who encourage others because they reap what they sow. They are continually being encouraged because they are always encouraging others. Jesus said that when you give to others, you are going to reap even more than you sow. Just giving a little encouragement to someone will come back to you in a lot more encouragement from others.

We say things like, "I'm just too shy. It's not my nature to go out of my way to encourage someone else." Yes, that's your old nature! But if you're going to be successful in life, you have to change. You have to be an encourager.

Everyone needs to be loved and appreciated. That's why it's important to praise and encourage others. Let them know they did a good job. Tell them how wonderful it is to spend time with them. Whether it is your spouse or your children or someone you work with, make sure they know how important they are to you.

People excel and grow when they are encouraged and praised. If you were encouraged and praised as you grew up, you are in a minority. Most of us were not. Most of us were raised with criticism and negativity, and we need to change. We need to stop that destructive cycle and raise our own children with praise and encouragement. That's one of the main ways you change your destiny and increase your happiness for years to come!

If you've never thought of yourself as a friendly "people person," who goes around making people feel good about themselves all the time, that's okay! You can do all things through Christ who strengthens you. Walking according to the Spirit and not the flesh is all about change. You need to make the decision to make some changes.

4. Get the focus off of you. Like the quote at the beginning of this chapter says, do you walk into a room expecting all eyes to be on you, or do you walk into a room and look to see who is there and how you can bless them? Are people a commodity to be used, to get you where you want to go; or are they your first concern because you want them to be happy and succeed?

When I first began in the ministry, I was a businessman. As a businessman, my focus was to get the job done. My attitude was that people were a problem. They kept me from getting where God was trying to take me. Obviously, when I became a pastor I had to change! I had to see people through God's eyes and love them the way He loves them. And most importantly, I had to realize that my agenda had become the people's agendas. In other words, by being their pastor—teaching them the Word, praying for them, blessing them in whatever way I could, and helping them succeed in life—I was fulfilling my destiny and calling.

When the focus is off you and onto others, when you are helping others reach their goals and fulfill their dreams, your goals and dreams will be realized. When you are more concerned with their happiness than yours, you will reap a harvest of happiness. Happiness matters.

On the other hand, if you push to achieve your goals, you'll run over people. You can love people without leading them, but you cannot lead people without loving them. You win people's hearts by helping them grow personally and by being concerned about their lives. They don't care how much you know until they know how much you care.

If you want to be happy, you have to forget about yourself and consider others first. If you're going to be a people person, you have to realize that it's not about you! It's about others.

5. What is in your heart determines your life. The Bible says, "For as he thinketh in his heart, so is he". The condition of your heart determines who you are, including whether or not you are a people person. Anytime someone doesn't feel good about themselves, they usually don't treat others very well. If somebody is not a people person, in their heart they probably don't like themselves.

If someone continuously strives for perfection, for example, they get depressed because no one can do anything good enough, including themselves. Or if they have a lot of pain in their heart, they will intentionally or unintentionally cause pain to others. Hurting people hurt people.

Jesus gave us three simple steps to healing a hurting heart. First, love the Lord your God with all your heart. Second, love your neighbor. Third, love yourself. When you love God with all of your heart, He fills your heart with love and life. He gives you the strength to forgive people who have hurt you and let go of your bitterness. Then you are able to love others. With a heart of love for God and love and forgiveness toward others, you can accept and love yourself.

None of this will happen if you don't put God first and love Him with all your heart. Your relationship with Him is the key to healing your heart, and your heart is the key to being a people person and fulfilling your destiny. Therefore, you must get your heart healed. As your relationship with the Lord grows, your relationship with people will grow.

Paul said that if you don't love people, you don't really love God.

Paul said that if you don't love people, you don't really love God. So if you find yourself despising someone, you had better back up and check your relationship with God. There are probably some negative cycles that need to be broken in your life when it comes to relationships.

Once you understand that your happiness is tied to the way you get along with others, you'll begin to face the hurts that are in your heart and let God heal you. And your whole life will change for the better if you do. Happiness matters.

6. You will never achieve greatness by yourself. No great thing has ever been accomplished by one person alone. Yes, inventive, new ideas come from single minds, but the manifestation of those ideas takes a lot of people. Progress is always achieved with teams. Obviously, you must be a people person and relate well with others to succeed in what God has called you to do.

There is a song that says, "One is the loneliest number that you'll ever know." Most of the greatest moments in our lives occur with other people. Being connected to others brings life's greatest joys. God didn't just save you and leave you alone. You are a member of the family of God, and the Bible says that every member is necessary for the body to function correctly.

Loners aren't happy people because God created us to be loving and social. He said that it wasn't good for us to be alone. He also said that believers should always fellowship with one another. If you have isolated yourself, I encourage you to make the effort to reach out to others and begin to fellowship with others.

Although it takes time and effort to build and maintain good relationships, it is worth it—and that leads to my final point.

7. Be a friend to make friends. Solomon, the wisest man in the world, wrote that the secret to having friends was being friendly. A people person spends their day making the conscious effort to bring peace and good will to everyone they meet. When they are in a group they don't stand off to the side and refuse to talk to anyone. They get in there and ask someone how they are doing and what's going on in their life.

Other than spending time with Jesus, being with people is the best cure for loneliness. Don't say, "Oh God, I'm so lonely," and sit in your apartment! Get out and get involved in your church. Join a small group that does things together outside of church. Volunteer at the clothing ministry or the homeless shelter. There are lots of opportunities to get to know people and do something that will help others at the same time.

You say, "But I'm just not comfortable meeting new people." I've got news for you. Most people are insecure in some way, and many of us feel a little nervous being around people we don't know very well. When you meet a new person, did you ever think about the fact that you are a new person to them too? They are probably a little nervous about you!

The point is, by being friendly to people you meet you make them feel secure and at ease. And when you put a person at ease, they like you for it! Because you were kind and nice to them, they want to be your friend. Friendly and loving people can find happiness no matter what is going on in their lives because their joy comes from seeing the happiness of others. They always have lots of friends. Happiness matters.

In conclusion . . . When you compliment someone from your heart, it makes them feel special, and we all want to feel special. We all need to be encouraged, to be loved and liked, and to know that we are not alone in this world. Every day we should find something good about somebody and go out of our way to encourage them.

If you want to be a people person, see to the needs of others before meeting your own needs. Take the focus off yourself and put it on someone else for a change. Be loving and friendly to everyone you meet. Put yourself in someone else's shoes before you judge them. And give love and encouragement at all times to all people.

There's an old saying, "All things being equal, the likeable person always wins. But all things not being equal, the likeable person still wins." The point is that you want to be the likeable person who wins! And what do you win? Happiness! Happiness matters. For further information contact www.HeritageChristianCenter.com.

Thought 12

THANKFULNESS AND HAPPINESS

Gratitude unlocks the fullness of life. It turns what we have into enough, and more. It turns denial into acceptance, chaos to order, confusion to clarity. It can turn a meal into a feast, a house into a home, a stranger into a friend. Gratitude makes sense of our past, brings peace for today, and creates a vision for tomorrow."

Melody Beattie

America celebrates giving thanks on a day called Thanksgiving. Our citizens take one day and thank God for all the things He has done for us and our families. But thanksgiving is not a one-day deal with believers in Jesus Christ. Thanksgiving is a way of life. Every single day we thank God for all He's done, all He's doing, and all He will do for us.

Being thankful, even for your trials and tribulations, draws you close to God and fills your heart with love and happiness. When you are grateful, you can be in the worst circumstances imaginable and be happy. That's why the Lord commands us to give thanks at all times for all things. Being happy is a natural consequence of being grateful to God for everything in our lives.

Give Thanks Always

Maybe before you gave your life to the Lord, you weren't thankful for anything. You took everything for granted and were a spoiled brat. Or maybe you were so beaten down that you never expected anything. Even when something good happened you never understood that God was blessing you or knew to give thanks. But now that you know the love of God, it should be the most normal thing to thank Him in everything.

Unfortunately, too many believers either never learn the importance of giving thanks or they begin taking God for granted and stop giving thanks. In some cases it's not that they don't love Him, but they just forget. That's why the Word of God tells us again and again how important it is to thank God in everything. David said, "I will bless the Lord at all times; His praise shall continually be in my mouth", and no one understood the power of giving thanks in all situations like he understood it. He had faced the lion and the bear before he picked up those five smooth stones to fight Goliath. He had a heart of thanksgiving when he said, "The Lord, who delivered me from the paw of the lion and from the paw of the bear, He will deliver me from the hand of this Philistine".

Giving thanks to God at all times and in all situations, praising Him continually, is one of the greatest weapons of our spiritual warfare. When we praise and thank God, we are sending the message that His power is operating in our lives and we are fully charged!

Everyone knows the story of Jonah and the great fish, but let me tell you "the rest of the story." God had told Jonah to go to Nineveh to preach the gospel, and Jonah had said, "No. I'm not going to go." Instead of obeying God, he got on a boat and went the other direction, so a terrible storm came upon the boat.

When everyone else found out that Jonah was the cause of the storm, they threw him overboard. So Jonah was hurled out of the boat, into the raging sea, only to be swallowed by a big fish. And while he was wrapped in seaweed in the belly of this fish, he said to God, "I will sacrifice to You with the voice of thanksgiving". Then God spoke to the fish, and the fish spit him up on the shore.

Like Jonah, having a heart of thanksgiving can save your life! The key is learning to put on a grateful heart even though you are in the pit of darkness and facing all hell. When your circumstances are terrifying and the situation is impossible, that is the time to raise your voice and give thanks to God. Nothing expresses your faith more than thanking God for all His blessings in the midst of a terrible crisis.

God wants us to have so much faith in Him that when things get tough we thank Him instead of complaining. The more we complain about something, the worse it gets; but the more we thank Him for His grace and mercy in the situation, the more His saving, healing, delivering power flows into our lives to set us free and keep us free.

Giving thanks to God always is a miracle-working phenomenon that accomplishes many wonderful things in your life. It keeps you safe, maintains happiness, and builds your faith.

Giving Thanks Increases Faith

Because we walk by faith and not by sight, we can continually give thanks to God, but giving thanks to God also increases our faith. We know He is going to work everything out for our good no matter what we are going through. We can still thank Him and praise Him for what He's doing. Our hearts are filled with gratitude, not attitude!

The nature of our flesh is completely self-centered, and when things go wrong or get uncomfortable the flesh always complains and gets worried and upset. That's having attitude in the midst of the storm, and attitude only makes matters worse.

Jesus understood that His faith rested in how grateful He was to His Father for everything. When his good friend Lazarus died, He traveled to his side. Jesus wept at the tomb. But before He commanded Lazarus to come forth—He said, "Father, I thank You that You have heard Me." Jesus gave thanks before He raised Lazarus from the dead!

Thanksgiving increases your faith because faith comes by hearing God's Word.

I don't know what's dead in your life, but you have to start with, "Father, I thank You." As you begin to thank Him for saving you, healing you, delivering you, hearing your prayers, providing for you, and protecting you—your faith will soar and you will have confidence to command what was dead to come forth!

Thanksgiving increases your faith because faith comes by hearing God's Word. When you hear God's promises with your own ears, coming out of your own mouth, your heart grabs hold of those powerful words and faith rises up. Your heart swells with faith when you give thanks to God.

Magnify the Lord Instead of Your Problems

David also said, "Oh magnify the Lord with me and let us exalt His Name together." He knew that God had to be a big God to get him through his messes and difficulties. You have the same assurance. You may not be able to change the situation that you're going through right now, but when you thank God He will give you the strength and wisdom to get through it.

If you are having some challenges on the job and begin to whine and complain to God about it, what happens? Nothing. In fact, it gets worse because whining and complaining invites the enemy into your life. But if you begin to thank God for the job and all the good things about it, not only is His wisdom and strength to handle the situation released in your life, but also His power is released into the lives of the people involved.

What I just described illustrates that giving thanks to God magnifies Him and His power in your life, but murmuring and complaining magnifies the problems in your life. I don't think you have to think too long about this to figure out what you want magnified in your life!

Having a heart of thanksgiving means magnifying God in all situations. As you praise Him and thank Him for all He has done and is doing and will do in your life, He gets bigger and bigger in your eyes. His presence surrounds you and He is all you can sense or feel or think about. You are operating in a principle that whatever you think about and talk about will multiply in your life. That's why the Bible tells us over and over again to give thanks instead of complaining.

God calls complaining an evil report because it magnifies the problem instead of Him. He also labels complaining doubt and unbelief because you complain when you have no faith in Him to help you. Complaining is never a good thing to do! It will stop you from receiving God's blessings and keep God from moving in your life.

One time I was complaining to God about something He did not do for me. He told me that He wasn't going to do one more thing for me until I was thankful for what He had already done. I learned in that situation that having a grateful heart was essential to seeing God move on my behalf. As I began to humbly thank Him and magnify His name, He got bigger and bigger and my complaints were forgotten.

You don't have to feel thankful to thank God and magnify the Lord, by the way. Being thankful is nothing more than obeying and trusting God. The truth is, magnifying the Lord in the midst of trying times is normal for a believer. It is the way God made us to speak and act. It is not normal to say, "Thank You, Jesus," when we are broke, our kids are running wild, and our spouse just ran off with someone else. That's why we need to thank God and magnify His name wherever we go and in all situations.

Prayer and Thanksgiving

Believers are not supposed to worry about anything. Instead, we are to pray about everything with a heart of thanksgiving. In Philippians 4:6, the Bible says, "Be anxious for nothing, but in everything by prayer and supplication, with thanksgiving, let your requests be made known to God." We are to earnestly seek God about the issues of our lives with thanksgiving in our hearts and mouths.

When you pray, you will either worry or give thanks. If you choose to thank God and tell Him how grateful you are for His presence and power in your life, eventually worry will just drop away. But if you choose to worry, eventually you will not be thankful for anything.

Worry kills gratitude, but a grateful heart dispels worry. You simply have to decide which way you are going to go. Heaven's gates will be closed to you as long as you are worrying and complaining. But they are open wide when you make your requests known with a heart of thanksgiving.

Even Jesus gave thanks when He made His requests known to God. When the disciples told Him that it was mealtime and the multitude He was ministering to were hungry, Jesus did not worry about it. He gave thanks! He took the little amount of bread and fish that He had, and He thanked His heavenly Father for it.

When you thank God for the little that you have, He will multiply it just like He did for Jesus. Jesus had five loaves of bread and two fish, but He was able to feed thousands of hungry men, women, and children with them.

What do you have in your hands? Thank God for it and watch Him multiply it! Miracles happen when you thank God. I believe you can turn your defeat into victory today if you enter His gates with thanksgiving and His courts with praise. He wants to do so much in your life and through your life! He is just waiting for you to come to Him and ask with a heart of thanksgiving.

Give Thanks and Get Happy

What are you grateful for today? I have so many things to be grateful for that I could spend my entire day thanking God. I had to learn to see my life through the eyes of thanksgiving instead of complaining, however. I had to learn to look at every issue and situation and thank God for what I had instead of complaining about what I didn't have.

Don't wait until God moves before you are thankful. Be thankful now. Thank Him for the things He's already done. You may be riding the bus to work and your mind wants to complain about it. But thank God you have two legs and the money you need to get on the bus.

Thank God for that little apartment you live in. There are some people living under bridges and in cardboard boxes who would love to live where you are living. Thank God for your spouse and all the wonderful qualities they possess. Thank Him for your children. There are many people in the world who have no one, no family or friends.

I am going to thank God for everything and concentrate on victory.

Do you know that you can even thank God for the government? In fact, you ought to be thankful you were born in the United States of America. You can read this book without being thrown in prison, and you have many opportunities and freedoms other people in the world don't have because you live here.

You cannot feel sorry for yourself for very long when you give thanks to God for everything in your life. I don't know about you, but I am through complaining about my needs and failures. I am going to thank God for everything and concentrate on victory. I'm going to encourage myself in the Lord. I've decided to have a radical heart of thanksgiving because I want to walk in God's miracle-working power.

When Jonah was caught in the belly of the fish, he gave thanks to God and the thing that had a hold of Jonah had to let him go. I don't know what problems have a hold of you right now, but if you'll put on a heart of thanksgiving, those things will have to turn you loose.

Having a heart of thanksgiving will get you free and keep you free. Maybe you are waiting for God to do something, but God's waiting for you to put on a heart of thanksgiving. You need to open your mouth say, "Thank You, Lord," and name everything He has done for you. Thank Him for being your Savior, your Father, your Comforter, your Deliverer, your Teacher, and the Friend that sticks closer than a brother. You will discover that you cannot have a heart of thanksgiving without being happy. Happiness matters. For more information contact **www.HeritageChristianCenter.com.**

Thought 13

JEALOUSY AND HAPPINESS

In jealousy there is more of self-love than of love to another.

Francois De La Rochefoucauld

I believe some of the unhappiest people in the world are those who are jealous of others. Jealousy eats away at their soul and steals their life. Although they can think of nothing but that other person and everything they have, all their thoughts and emotions are selfish and self-centered. They want what that person has, and they hate them for having what they believe they should have.

Even believers can fall prey to envying other people, coveting what they have, or being suspicious of a friend's or loved one's loyalty to them. In order to be happy and stay happy in this life, we have to be on guard that we never fall into this terrible trap of jealousy.

Shakespeare and the Bible Agree

In his famous play, *Othello*, William Shakespeare called jealousy the "the green-eyed monster," and that is what people still call it today. It is interesting that James says, "But if you have bitter jealousy and selfish ambition in your heart, do not be arrogant and so lie against the truth. This wisdom is not that which comes down from above, but is earthly, natural, demonic. For where jealousy and selfish ambition exist, there is disorder and every evil thing."

The Bible says that jealousy lies against the truth. It is earthly, natural, and demonic. And it causes disorder and every evil thing. I would say that the Bible just described a green-eyed monster! Therefore, we can be confident that we are being biblically correct when we say that jealous people have been captured by the green-eyed monster.

James tells us that anytime there is jealousy or selfish ambition in our hearts, pride and arrogance will cause us to lie against the truth. In other words, instead of admitting we have a problem with the green-eyed monster, our pride rises up and we lie about it. We step out of the truth and into deception.

When jealousy operates in someone's life, you also see pride and deception. If you've ever known someone who is jealous, you have probably sensed that they were just not seeing things as they really were. When you tried to reason with them, even if they considered what you were saying, you saw that they preferred to believe what they wanted to believe instead of the truth. Pride and jealousy work together to deceive.

> *Where jealousy exists, there is going to be every evil thing.*

Where jealousy exists, there is going to be every evil thing. Jealous people bring pain and heartache to everyone they touch because they are so deceived by selfish ambition that they become mean and cruel.

Jealousy is all about me. I want more than my brothers and sisters have. I want my ministry to be more famous than another minister's. I want a bigger house and a more expensive car than my friends'. I want to look better than anyone else in the room. I want to be the center of attention at the party. I want to win all the awards and be the most gifted person in the universe. I want to be in control wherever I go.

There is only one way to deal with jealousy. The moment it shows up in a thought or a feeling, we must get rid of it immediately.

Give the Boot to the Green-Eyed Monster!

No matter who we are, we all get hit with jealousy from time to time. There are not many individuals who are so secure in who they are that they never have an envying or jealous thought. No one wants to admit that they are having a problem with the green-eyed monster. Instinctively human beings know how negative it is, so they don't want to tell anyone that they have a jealous thought.

We should be humble and say, "I have to admit that I got jealous when she decided to ask him for counsel instead of me." But instead we say things like, "I'm not jealous. I'm just territorial. I'm just possessive. I'm just protecting what is mine." The truth of the matter is that it's a jealousy issue.

If you're going to be happy you must deal with your baggage, and jealousy is very heavy luggage! Here is how it works. You love something a whole lot. Because you love it so much, you feel like you possess it. It becomes yours, which is a mistake right there because everything you have belongs to God. If you can live in the truth that everything and everyone in your life are God's and not yours, it will be much easier for you to defeat jealousy in your life.

If you "take possession" of what you love and forget that it belongs to God; when it slips through your fingers and somebody else has it, jealousy will take over. What you love could be your house, a position at work, or a person. Whatever it is and no matter how much it means to you, don't give in to jealousy!

Jealousy Means Torment and Death

If you don't immediately kick jealousy out of your life, it will bring torment and death. It can be excruciatingly painful to lose something or someone you love to someone else. Then you associate your pain with that person. They have what you should have, so you begin to hate them. Jealousy always will lead to hatred and eventually to murder.

Statistics show that a large percentage of murders take place among families and people who know one another. That is because jealousy is stronger the more you care about something or someone. Jealousy has caused murder since the Fall. The first murder in human history took place in the beginning, when Cain was jealous of his brother Abel and killed him. We see the green-eyed monster at work throughout the Bible.

Joseph was Jacob's favorite son, so his brothers were jealous and tried to kill him. If one of his brothers had not intervened, they would have killed him. The prodigal son left home and lived like the devil, and the good son stayed home and didn't cause his daddy any trouble. But the dad opened his arms to the wayward son when he came home, and the "good son" got jealous.

Miriam was jealous of her brother Moses. She had saved his life as a child and had sung a song of the Lord after they crossed the Red Sea, but one day jealousy rose up in her and she said, "Does God only speak through Moses? Can't He speak through me as well?" God removed His hand of protection, and she was struck with leprosy. But Moses prayed and interceded to God for her, and she was healed. I wonder how many people are sick and dying because of jealousy?

I wonder how many people are sick and dying because of jealousy?

When King Saul recognized that the Spirit of God had left him and was now on David, and that the people were singing, "Saul has killed his thousands and David his ten thousands", jealousy took hold of his heart and he began to hate David. It didn't take long before he tried to murder David, and he continued to try to kill David until he died. Saul's life was destroyed by jealousy.

The religious leaders were jealous of Jesus, and the Bible says that "the chief priests had handed Him over because of envy" Jealousy put Jesus on the cross!

When jealousy resides in the heart of a person, they are in such torment that their whole demeanor changes. They will say and do things that they would never normally do—including murder. Jealousy is destructive and dangerous.

Take Off the Mask

Before you can get rid of jealousy, you must admit you have it. That may seem obvious, but as I have said before, few people want to admit that they have even had a jealous thought. The following questions will help you to recognize jealousy.

- Is it hard for you to compliment other people?
- Are you territorial?
- Every time a certain person's name is mentioned, do you wish something bad would happen to them?
- If anyone else says anything nice about a certain person, do you point out all their negative traits?
- Are you extremely possessive?
- Do you criticize people who excel beyond you?
- Are you always competitive?
- Are you constantly comparing yourself to others?
- Do you always want to know what everyone else is doing, buying, and who they are associating with?
- Do you distrust those you really care about and continually check up on them?

When our church was in a little storefront building, I worked so hard knocking on doors and doing everything I could to minister to the people. But I never seemed to get anywhere. Other pastors in the city were succeeding, and I was jealous. It got so bad that I would go to pastors' conferences and come home depressed. I was beginning to be tormented by it.

I began to search my soul and discovered I was jealous of other pastors' success. I had to crucify a lot of pride to admit it, and I'm glad I did.

The reason jealousy is so ugly is because it was part of the original sin of Lucifer. He literally embodied jealousy and became Satan, the enemy of God. Jealousy rebelled against God. That's why we must be honest with ourselves, admit to any thought of jealousy, and rip that mask off our face. If we don't, jealousy is evil and will lead to the death of our soul.

Getting Rid of Jealousy Forever

After you have taken the mask off and admitted you have a problem with jealousy, what do you do? The first thing you have to do is repent. "Oh God, I see that I have allowed that ugly, green-eyed monster to operate in me. Forgive me, because I know it is wrong."

The Bible says that the wages of sin is death, and God is against anything that will hurt you. He is not trying to keep you from having fun or "just being honest about what you are feeling and thinking." He wants to keep you safe and happy by keeping sin out of your life.

The second thing you have to do is pray for the person or persons you have been jealous of. At first it may be awkward and even bring up negative emotions, but if you just keep praying for them, God will change your heart and replace the jealousy with love.

Jealousy is the opposite of love. That's why jealousy is a love issue for believers. You cannot really love someone and be jealous of them. First Corinthians 13:4 says that love is not jealous. Jealousy focuses on selfish desires, but love wants others to be blessed.

The third thing you need to do to defeat jealousy and be happy is to begin to celebrate other people's victories with them and go out of your way to compliment people. When they are blessed, you are blessed. Make an effort to look for the best in people and say, "You did a great job with that." Or, "You look terrific today."

If the situation calls for it, forgive those who have hurt you by taking what was yours, whether it was your video game or your spouse. To defeat jealousy and be happy, you must walk in forgiveness and love.

And finally, remember who you are in Christ. When you are secure in who you are in Him, you will not be jealous of what other people have or do. You won't get jealous of your neighbor, even though he bought the car you wanted, because you are of a royal priesthood and a holy nation.

The world and your flesh will try to get you into competition in every area of your life, to continually compare yourself with others. Comparing yourself with others always opens the door to pride, jealousy, and hate because there will always be someone who is better, stronger, wiser, more talented, better looking, richer, more successful, and better liked than you are. It leads to nothing but discouragement, depression, jealousy, and self-loathing.

The Bible says that comparing yourself with others is not wise. It is not wise because nobody can be as good at being you as you can! God never called you to be like somebody else. He called you to be an original and not a copy. He has a specific plan that is tailor-made for your personality, your mind and heart, your gifts and talents, and even your physical body. You are unique and have a special role to play in God's kingdom that no one else can play.

When you dwell on your heavenly Father's unconditional love and absolute goodness toward you and love Him with your whole heart, the green-eyed monster has no entrance to your life. And, as a result, the happiness in your heart will spill over into the lives of others. Happiness matters. For more teaching materials contact us at **www.HeritageChristianCenter.com.**

Thought 14

THE FRUSTRATION OF LONELINESS

The most terrible poverty is loneliness and the feeling of being unloved.

Mother Teresa

We all can get frustrated when we are trying to pay our bills, get along with a spouse or friend, please our employers, and raise our children to be decent human beings. We become frustrated in the day-to-day grind when everything planned goes awry and life seems completely out of our control. But one of the most frustrating things we deal with as human beings is loneliness.

It is no coincidence that the very first thing God called "not good" is being alone. The Bible says, "And the LORD God said, 'It is not good that man should be alone; I will make him a helper comparable to him'". From the beginning we were never to be alone, and we were never to be lonely.

Filling the Void Within

Loneliness is one of mankind's greatest problems. The truth is that we are born with an empty spot inside us that only God can fill. When we give our lives to the Lord, our hearts are satisfied with His love, peace, and joy. But it isn't long before we experience a challenge in life, such as our first child going to college or the death of a loved one. Then loneliness tries to come into our lives and steal our happiness.

We can be attacked with loneliness anytime we think that something is missing in our lives.

We can be attacked with loneliness anytime we think that something is missing in our lives. Loneliness creeps into your soul when something you long for is not there or broken, and loneliness can be devastating if you don't deal with it.

I believe that we are living in the loneliest society that's ever existed. Loneliness affects the rich and the poor, every culture, and every profession—from the janitor in the basement to the pilot in an airplane. Loneliness affects the married and the unmarried, and every color of people.

One of the biggest deceptions of the enemy today is that marriage will solve your loneliness problem. Not only does marriage not cure loneliness, but it can cause loneliness! Sometimes the worst case of loneliness comes after you marry the person of your dreams and everything is not exactly the way you pictured it.

Loneliness comes in when you do not communicate and nurture each other in a relationship. Each person has a responsibility to tell the other what is going on in their lives and how they are thinking and feeling about it. You can't expect the other person to know everything about you, even if you have been married for many years.

Our lifestyles can cause loneliness. We're spending more and more time on airplanes, watching television, surfing the Internet, and playing video games or watching movies. The less time we spend with human beings, the greater the possibility for loneliness to grab hold of us.

More and more people are working at home, and this can be good or bad. If they live in a family where the children come home in the afternoon and the other spouse comes home at dinner time, working at home can be a great thing. But if they are single and live alone in a house, don't know their neighbors, and don't have any family in town, after awhile they may feel like they are in solitary confinement.

Think about this. Even God has never been alone. The Father, the Son, and the Holy Spirit have always existed as one. Adam walked and talked with them every day. But there was still something not right. Mankind was made in God's image, but not exactly like Him. God said it wasn't good for Adam to be one of His kind, so He created Eve, the perfect soul mate and partner for him.

The conclusion we come to is that God never meant for us to be alone. If there are no human beings around, He is there. When we are born again and become His child, He places us in the body of Christ and tells us not to neglect fellowship with the other members of His body. He created us to be a vital part of His Church. For believers, the local church is where we get rid of any loneliness in our lives by loving one another, caring for one another, meeting each other's needs, and encouraging each other in the faith.

Every member of the body of Christ is a minister of reconciliation, and you cannot minister if you don't fellowship with other believers and get out in the world to reconcile other people to God through Jesus Christ. Also, no one can minister to you if you are by yourself all the time. If you are isolated and a loner, you are missing God's plan for your life.

We must have fellowship with God and fellowship with the saints to remain strong in the faith and overcome the frustration of loneliness. Only God can fill the void within, and only intimacy with Him and other believers will keep it filled.

Causes of Loneliness

1. Major changes cause loneliness. We don't like change because it means either giving something up or letting something go. Any transition in life involves dealing with the unknown and leaving the familiar and comfortable. That kind of change can bring loneliness. Losses, disappointments, and new experiences can all bring loneliness.

Do you remember how you felt when you walked into that big building on your first day of school or the first day at a new job? Remember the first time you visited your church? Everything seemed so overwhelming. You didn't know anybody. It was very intimidating. You had to fight the feeling of being alone.

2. Being separated from those we love can cause loneliness. This doesn't just happen to the business person when they are away from their family on a business trip or to the grandmother who lives across country from her children and grandchildren. Because of the breakdown in the family today, kids are left alone a tremendous amount of the time. That is why so many kids are lonely, and loneliness can cause them to do crazy and destructive things.

Some kids join gangs to feel a sense of family. Many are having sex simply because they are desperate for any kind of love or affection. Some get on the computer and become obsessed with pornography, ungodly life-styles and music. It is becoming more and more evident that tragedies such as the killings at Columbine High School are related to what kids are exposed to on the Internet. They do all these things not to feel lonely. They want to belong. They want to feel important.

People who travel a lot in their business are especially vulnerable to loneliness because they are separated from family and friends on a regular basis. Have you ever been in a strange town and walked into a hotel room and felt loneliness fill your soul? This is when people get hooked on pornography or begin to drink or use drugs to get them through the time away from home when they are alone.

I learned awhile ago that when I travel, I need to have somebody with me. This not only keeps me accountable, but it also keeps me from getting lonely.

3. When people reject us it can cause loneliness. Remember when you were a kid and the other kids would gang up on you and say hurtful things. That created loneliness in your life. The old saying, "Sticks and stones may break my bones but words will never hurt me," is a lie. Bones will heal but only God can heal a heart that has been wounded by unkind and cruel words.

Rejection is something we all experience, but that doesn't mean it is any easier to take. When people don't want to talk to us or be around us, especially if we love them or have great respect for them, it can be extremely painful. It feels as though everyone we care about has forsaken us and brings terrible loneliness. If the pain of rejection is too great, we will build walls around our lives and become even more lonely.

> *Rejection is something we all experience, but that doesn't mean it is any easier to take.*

If that describes you, Jesus came to heal your broken heart. But you have to trust Him with your life and begin opening up to Him and other believers who will pray for you and stand with you. If you don't, you will miss your purpose and calling in life.

4. Not receiving the love and acceptance we need causes loneliness. God created us to be loved and accepted. If we don't get it first from God and then from other human beings, we will go to great lengths to get it. We become alcoholics. We become drug addicts. We become workaholics. We have sex with anyone who wants us because we believe they really want us for ourselves. We try materialism, thinking that things will fill the void. The flesh always tells us we can buy our way to happiness. But none of these things satisfy us.

How to Handle Loneliness

We've seen what the problem is. Now I'm going to give you five things to do when loneliness hits you hard.

1. Draw closer to the Lord. He is the vine and you are the branch. He is your life-line, where you get your strength, courage, wisdom, and power to live. When you go through a major change, are separated from your loved ones, are rejected, and no one is giving you the love and acceptance you need; that is when you draw everything you need from Him.

Only Jesus can meet your needs, and He wants to meet them! He wants to be your doctor, lawyer, counselor, and friend. Talk to Him, listen to Him, and be totally honest with Him. (He knows it all anyway!) He never gets tired of you, and you will never feel lonely with Him.

Sometimes when you get hurt and feel all alone, you step away from the Lord. That is the worst thing you can do! He is the source of all the love you need. You will not find it in your friends or your family. Only Jesus can give you the pure, holy, everlasting unconditional love and acceptance you crave. And when you receive it from Him every day, you will never be lonely.

2. Break your isolation. Another way of saying this is: Join a church family. God never intended for you to be alone. If you have isolated yourself, especially from other believers, then you are in a dangerous place. You may just be lonely today, but tomorrow it could get much, much worse. Find a place to serve and start connecting with others. The best way to do that is to get involved in one of the ministries of the church and get to know the other people involved. Let them get to know you too. Tear down any walls you have built around yourself. Pray and ask God where He wants you to be and then get there!

No great man or woman of God liked to be alone, even Jesus. That's why He asked the disciples to be with Him in the Garden of Gethsemane, just before He was crucified. He didn't want to be alone. Paul never went anywhere alone, and when he came to a new town he always stayed with a family. So why do you think it wise for you to be alone?

You might remember the story of the little girl who got scared during a thunderstorm one night. She ran into her parents' bedroom and jumped in bed with them. Her father said, "Baby, don't you know that Jesus is with you?"

She said, "Yes Daddy, I know He's with me, but right now I need somebody with skin on them to hug me."

All of us need someone with skin on to give us a godly hug and affection, especially if we live alone. Hang out with believers who will love you and watch your loneliness melt away.

3. Use your time wisely. In other words, don't sit around and feel sorry for yourself, complaining to God how lonely you are. Take action! Get out of the house and be productive. Reach out and touch someone. Use your time to bless and serve someone who is lonelier and more alone than you are. Make some quality changes in your life so that you don't waste your life.

Anytime you focus on yourself, loneliness will be the result.

4. Forgive those who have hurt you. When someone hurts you, don't withdraw from everyone else. Forgive instantly and let it roll off of you. Give it to the Lord, and let Him handle the person who offended you. If you allow yourself to wallow in self-pity and hold a grudge, you will become bitter and lonely. And no one likes to be around a bitter, angry person. That's why you will isolate yourself and cause even more loneliness if you refuse to forgive.

5. Focus on others. Anytime you focus on yourself, loneliness will be the result. The loneliest people in the world are self-centered. God made us to be cheerful givers and grateful receivers not selfish takers. When you are self-centered, you are consumed with having other people meet your needs. As a result, you are not going to get very much in return. But if you focus on meeting the needs of others and giving to them, praying for them, and loving them, any loneliness in your life will simply disappear. You will be so happy having a blast blessing others that you won't even think about yourself! Happiness matters.

A Final Word

It was discovered during World War II that you could break soldiers by isolating them. They became unstable, uncertain, and terribly insecure. That's why the enemy will try to isolate you from other people, especially other believers. He wants to break you and make you useless in the kingdom of God. He wants to destroy your life and your happiness. Don't let the enemy break you.

You may be feeling so lonely today that you would like to end it all. You may believe nobody cares about you or wants you. But Jesus does. And He understands the pain of loneliness. He felt it when He faced His greatest challenge and temptation in the Garden of Gethsemane. He knew He would have to endure the cross alone, that even

God would forsake Him. Then He took all your loneliness on the cross.

Now He is standing in front of you saying, "Why are you holding onto it? Give it to Me. Let me fill your soul with My happiness and peace." Happiness matters. For more encouragement go to **www.HeritageChristianCenter.com.**

Thought 15

WHEN YOU'RE AT THE BREAKING POINT

Take the most difficult challenge you are now facing and turn it into the greatest opportunity to grow simply by changing how you see it. Dead ends then become turning points.

Bob Perks

Marriage. Children. Work. Church. Ministry. Finances. Health. Recreation. Hobbies. Vacation. Parents. Neighbors. House. Yard. Pets. Cars. Boats. Buses. Planes. Trains. These are all things we deal with, sometimes on a daily basis—and it all adds up to stress.

In the eighth chapter I talked about the fast pace of life in this world and how we need to get into God's rhythm of life by simplifying our lives. But what happens when everything that can go wrong goes wrong and your life spins completely out of control? What do you do when you're at the breaking point in your life?

Stress and Responsibility

You have to have some level of stress in your life or else you're dead. It takes a certain amount of stress to be able to get some things done. For example, before a violin can make music you've got to put stress on the strings by pulling them tight. The same thing is true for people. A little bit of stress causes us to get our life in order and our adrenaline flowing so that we can accomplish what we need to accomplish.

On the other hand, if you pull the strings too tight, they will snap. Like the strings, human beings need just the right amount of tension to produce the right sound. Too much tension in our lives will cause us to snap.

We all know that too much stress in our lives will bring us to a breaking point. Everyone knows someone or has heard of someone who lost it or had a breakdown. We don't think about it happening to ourselves, however, and we just keep going at a breakneck pace. We are often blind to the fact that we are wearing ourselves out spiritually, mentally, emotionally, and physically.

When you're at a breaking point, it just feels like you're about to explode. All you can see is that everything in your life is falling apart. That was the way Elijah felt after he took on the prophets of Baal and sat down to die. He had seen God do miracle after miracle, and yet he told God he was the only one in Israel who was serving Him and he wanted to die.

Elijah didn't get from calling God's fire down from heaven and stopping the rain for three years, to thoughts of suicide without some stress and dysfunction in his life. He was taking responsibility on himself that was not his. He had given God's Word to the people, and when they didn't live it the way he thought they should, he felt responsible. He based his success on whether or not the children of Israel followed the Lord.

You cannot be responsible for other people's decisions!

If you haven't already heard this, then what I'm about to tell you is going to set you free.

You cannot be responsible for other people's decisions!

I get up several times a week and give my congregation the Word of God, but I can't take responsibility for how they live their lives. If I preach on holiness on Sunday, and Monday I'm in a restaurant and hear one of our members swearing at a waitress, I cannot blame myself and get upset. I cannot judge them. I can only forgive them, pray for them, ask God for the strength not to fall into the same temptation—and if the Holy Spirit leads just drop by to say a friendly hello on my way out!

You have to do the same thing with your parents, your spouse, your children, your work associates, your ministry partners, and your neighbors. If you don't get anything else get this: *You are only responsible for you because you can only make your own decisions.* One of the leading causes of breakdowns is taking on too much responsibility. That's why we need to know where our boundaries are with other human beings.

If I took responsibility for how every member of our congregation lived I would be dead in an hour. There is no way I could carry all those burdens and run all those lives. Yet many pastors, fathers and mothers, employers and employees, teachers and mentors do just that. And eventually they break down.

Set godly, healthy boundaries in your life. Jesus said to love each other, to avoid sin, to beware of the enemy and his schemes, and to worship God with all your heart. The Holy Spirit lives inside you, but even He has God-given boundaries.

The Holy Spirit doesn't make you do anything. He puts you in remembrance of God's Word and leaves the decision to you. He gives you a check in your spirit that what you are thinking of saying is not right, but the words can still come out of your mouth if you don't choose to stop them. He knows that to be like Jesus, you have to say, "Not my will, Father, but Your will be done in my life." He cannot say it for you or make you say it because if He does you will never become like Jesus.

Somebody said once, "Give your loved ones the dignity of making their own mistakes and learning from them." If you are always getting into someone else's business, you are not only going to burn out but you are hindering God from working in their lives. Oooooooh! We don't like to hear that, but it's true.

Ask the Holy Spirit to show you how much to get involved in other people's lives, including your loved ones, and don't take responsibility for them. They belong to God, not you!

How to Get Past the Breaking Point

No matter how bad it looks or what the doctor, lawyer, or accountant has told you, it is never as bad as it seems. How do I know this? I have been there! And God is always greater than the mess we are in.

If you feel that it's not worth going on and you might as well throw in the towel, I have five things that will get you past your breaking point and back on track with the Lord again. Maybe you want to leave your ministry, your job, your spouse, your children, or even end it all and kill yourself. Don't do it! Read on and allow the Holy Spirit to minister to you. And as you read, I want you to remember what the Bible tells you. "Many are the afflictions [or the troubles] of the righteous, but the Lord shall deliver him out of them all."

Jesus is in the deliverance business. It means He's in your life to get you through Red Seas, help you to walk on water, and get you to the other side of your breaking point so you can be happy and productive in life. Happiness matters.

1. Release your frustration. When you're at your breaking point, frustration is at an all-time high. You're so frustrated with everyone and everything that you're even frustrated with God. So the first thing you have to do is release your frustration and deal head-on with all the negative emotions stirring inside of you.

Emotions like fear, worry, guilt, depression, anger, bitterness, and grief can be overwhelming anytime you feel like you're about to break. The natural tendency is to hold on to them and isolate yourself, but God wants you to give it all to Him. He wants you to let it go. The Bible says in Psalm 62:8, "Pour out your heart before Him. God is a refuge for us."

Tell Jesus how you feel and what you are thinking. Lay it all out for Him: your fears, your worries, your doubts, your anger, your sorrow—all of it—even why you are mad at Him, if you are. If you don't open up and allow all your frustration to pour out on Jesus, one day it will explode on someone else, and probably someone you love.

> *Tell Jesus how you feel and what you are thinking.*

The other day I was on an airplane and the flight attendant dropped a can of soda. It hit the floor and exploded all over the cabin. The ceiling, the walls, and the people were covered with sticky soda. That's what will happen to you if you don't release everything to Jesus. One day someone will drop you and you will explode.

Through the book of Psalms David pours his heart out to God. Psalm after psalm he will begin by releasing all his fears and telling all his troubles, but by the end of the psalm he is rejoicing in the Lord. Why? He released his frustration to the Lord.

2. Don't become bitter. Reaching a breaking point means you are on your last nerve because someone has let you down again and again, it's been years and God still hasn't moved, or you have tithed and given offerings and you still cannot pay all your bills. Under these circumstances, it is easy to just begin to seethe and get bitter.

The problem is that bitterness doesn't help you, it makes things worse. When bitterness sets in, it can destroy the relationship with the person who let you down, it drives you right out of the will and presence of God, and it cuts off all His blessings in your life. Bitterness will destroy you.

The truth is that life is never easy. If you are waiting for all of your troubles to go away before you become happy, you will never be happy. They are never going to stop. But if you refuse to get bitter and trust the Lord instead, your life will get better. You will begin to deal with trouble more wisely.

The opposite of bitterness is gratitude, so the antidote to bitterness is thanking God. You can turn from bitterness to gratitude by just thanking Him for all the good things He's done, is doing, and will do for you. You don't have to feel like it! You just do it, and do it again, and again, until you drive bitterness out of your life. You can be happy if you put on a heart of thanksgiving.

"Thank You, Lord, that you got me out of the bars. Thank You, Lord, that I'm on my way to heaven. Thank You, Lord, that You are the Lord of my life and I'm never alone." First Thessalonians 5:18 says that no matter what happens, always be thankful, for this is God's will for your life. We're not thankful that we had some losses; we're just thankful that God is with us in the loss. And there's something about a voice of thanksgiving that causes God to show up and miracles to happen.

3. Reach out for help. When you reach your breaking point you will be tempted to pull yourself into a little shell. You don't want anybody to know how bad things are or that you are in such bad shape. You don't want anyone touching you or talking to you because they might just hurt you more than you're already hurting. So you throw yourself a great pity party and just wallow in your self-made fortress of explosive emotions.

Whether you're rich, smart, "the right color and nationality," or have it all together; I've got news for you. You still have a breaking point, and when you reach it you cannot get through it by yourself. When you get distraught over life, you won't see things correctly. Your perspective gets distorted. That's why you need another set of eyes and ears and brains—and someone else's spiritual wisdom—to help you.

God designed the body of Christ to heal itself, which means we all need to do our part, stay connected to one another, and allow the other parts to minister to us when we need it. I need you to pray with me when I get to my breaking point, and you need me to pray with you when you get to your breaking point. We are in this together.

During hurricane Katrina, a tidal surge carried eight dolphins out of their aquarium and into the ocean. They were domesticated and didn't know how to hunt, but because they stayed together they were found and rescued. If any of them had gone off by themselves, their chances of being saved would have been drastically diminished.

The enemy's strategy is to drive you crazy and isolate you so that he can destroy you, but if you will swallow your pride and reach out to others, you can be loved, prayed for, encouraged, built up in your faith, and even have a laugh or two.

4. Get your eyes on the Lord and off yourself. At the breaking point all you can see is you and your problems. That's when you have to turn to Jesus and worship Him. Worship Him until you have poured everything you've got into Him. Then listen to what He says.

Most likely, after He comforts you, He will send you on an errand to comfort someone else. "Blessed be the God and Father of our Lord Jesus Christ, the Father of mercies and God of all comfort, who comforts us in all our tribulation, that we may be able to comfort those who are in any trouble, with the comfort with which we ourselves are comforted by God".

When Elijah was depressed, the Lord told him to get out of his cave and go minister to someone else. He knew Elijah was consumed with himself and his problems, and part of his deliverance was helping someone else get delivered of the same thing! He was encouraging Elijah to participate in his own deliverance.

> *I want you to know that God has great plans for your life.*

When you minister to others what the Holy Spirit is ministering to you, you change your focus from yourself and what you are going through to God and what He's doing in you and through you. You take yourself off the throne and put Him back on the throne of your heart.

5. Don't give up. Jeremiah says, "I know the plans that I have for you, says the Lord, plans to prosper you and not to harm you. Plans to give you hope and a future." Aren't you glad you serve a God that has plans to prosper you and give you a great future?

I want you to know that God has great plans for your life. He has a purpose for you that goes beyond the trouble you're going through today. I've been there, and I know that He is keeping track of everything that you're going through. The more unfair and unjust it is, the more He'll multiply blessings back to you if you don't give up and keep moving forward in faith.

Every time you reach a breaking point it is a test. You have before you a series of choices that will add up to either quitting or persevering through to victory. Paul's life was a story of great persistence and a great example for us.

He was jailed in chains, beaten, whipped, stoned, left for dead, run out of town, shipwrecked, and a deadly snake bit him. He admitted that he was pressed on every side, way beyond what he thought he could bear, but he still persevered. At the end of his life he said, "I have fought the good fight, I have finished the race, I have kept the faith".

No matter what is happening, how you feel, or what the situation is—it's not over until God says it's over. But just like there are times when an athlete has to run with pain in order to win, there's going to be times in your life that you have to hang onto Jesus and keep going no matter how you feel.

Runners use the expression "hitting the wall", when they are so physically exhausted that everything within them says to quit. They feel like they'll die if they take one more step. But they know if they press through the pain they'll get a second wind and the pain will be overwhelmed by the sheer pleasure of running.

When you hit the wall is when you are on the verge of your breakthrough. You always come to a breaking point before you see a breakthrough. So don't quit! Your happiest moments are just ahead of you. Happiness Matters. For additional help contact us at www.HeritageChristianCenter.com.

Thought 16

PRAISE YOUR WAY TO HAPPINESS

To praise God in the midst of dire circumstances is happiness beyond all calculation, for praise is faith's certainty that the Almighty will crush the impossible with the miraculous.

Sinclair Meid

It is vital that we praise God for every blessing in our lives. We must never get happy and forget who made us happy. That's why the apostle Paul exhorted us to rejoice in the Lord always. We must never forget that He is the One who blesses us, prospers us, and gives us inner peace and happiness.

Praising the Lord is not hard when your life is going well, but it is hard to praise Him when your life is turned upside down. I'm talking about praising Him when you're going through hell. You must choose to rejoice whether it is feast or famine. Trust Him and give Him glory no matter how bad things get. Why? There's something about praising God that will lift the burdens off of your shoulders.

Praise Him driving down the highway. Praise Him doing the dishes and vacuuming the house—and that you have a house! Praise Him when you're cutting the grass. Praise Him when you get laid off. Praise Him when the rent is due. Praise him when your best friend betrays you. You can praise your way to happiness.

There's something about praising God that will lift the burdens off of your shoulders.

In 2 Chronicles 20 we read the account of King Jehoshaphat and the nation of Judah. Several ungodly nations were ready to attack them, so they all fasted and sought the Lord for help. In verse 15 (my paraphrase) the Lord answered, "Do not be afraid or dismayed because the battle is not yours. It is Mine."

When the Lord spoke, Jehoshaphat got a revelation of how that battle would be won. His strategy was to set the praisers right in front of all the troops. The Bible says in verse 22, "Now when they began to sing and to praise, the Lord set ambushes against the people of Ammon, Moab, and Mount Seir, who had come against Judah; and they were defeated."

When you praise God He will fight the thing that's fighting you, just like he did for Jehoshaphat.

Praise Stops the Enemy

There's something about praising the Lord that stops the enemy in his tracks, and it's called the presence and power of God. God inhabits the praises of His people.

Every time I lift my hands to the Lord, I'm saying to all my weaknesses and faults, "By the Blood of Jesus Christ, you are defeated in my life." Every time I clap my hands in praise, I'm claiming victory over sin, sickness, hell, and the grave in His glorious name.

David was a psalmist before he became a warrior and a king. He defeated Goliath with only a slingshot because he knew how to praise the Lord. Like David, you don't have to have an army to defeat your giants. All you need is a little slingshot with a good hallelujah behind it!

Christians are always saying the word hallelujah, but do you know how powerful that word is? Hallelujah is a combination of two Hebrew words, *halal* and *Yahh*. *Halal* means "shine; hence, to make a show, to boast; and thus to be (clamorously) foolish; to celebrate." *Yahh* is short for Jehovah.[1]

When you cry, "Hallelujah!" you are making a scene for the Lord! You are shining in His glory, boasting of His mighty power, and celebrating who He is. You are also inviting God to move in your life. Your praise declares that the enemy is not welcome and Jesus is Lord. As a result, miraculous things happen.

The enemy attacked Paul and Silas when they were serving God. They were thrown into prison in chains for preaching the gospel. Instead of whining and begging God for help, they began to sing His praises. As their praises went up, their chains fell off, the prison doors flew open!

God is no respecter of persons, and what He did for Paul and Silas and David, He will do for you. Nothing in life can intimidate you when you live a life of praise as they did. When praise is continually on your lips, the enemy will not want to be around you because God is there.

Praise Is the Language of Faith

When you get into an impossible situation and enter into praise, you are declaring, "Father, I trust You to take care of me and all that concerns me. This is Your fight, and You will deliver me." Praise expresses your faith in God.

There's a story about a church mother who would praise God for one hour and then take one minute to ask God for the things she needed. She would praise Him for

His excellent greatness, for all the things He had done in her life, for His goodness and mercy that endures forever, and for being her mighty God. Then she spent just one minute saying, "Lord, I need some help."

This woman not only loved God; she had godly wisdom. She knew God was pleased when she had faith in Him and so she spent an hour in His presence, building her faith by praising Him. Then, in that one minute of making her requests known to Him, she spoke with total confidence that He was willing and able to meet all her needs. She understood that praise was the language of faith.

Praise Is Total Surrender

The *New American Standard Bible* says that God is "enthroned" upon the praises of His people. When you praise God you literally build a chair for Him to sit on in your heart. You are asking Him to reign in your life.

When you don't praise God, you make no place for Him in your heart, and you will not sense His presence. That's why I praise Him at all times and in all situations. I want Him to be enthroned in my life so I can feel His presence and do His will.

Our natural minds will tell us not to praise God if we are depressed, discouraged, or things aren't going well. Our flesh says, "Just sit there. Stew in it. Feel sorry for yourself. You need a break, so just do whatever you feel like doing." But that's the exact opposite of what we're supposed to do!

When we get down, the only way to get back up is to surrender to God, to throw up our hands and praise Him. After all, our lives are not our own. They are His. When we surrender totally to Him and praise Him, He shows up and what seemed impossible becomes possible.

Praise Brings Miracles on the Scene

When we make a joyful noise unto the Lord miracles begin to happen. I have seen believers who didn't know much about God praise Him, and miracles flowed in their lives. The one thing they did know, however, was to praise God no matter what they were going through. It brought His joy into their hearts when they faced difficult or impossible situations.

We often think of joy as simply a nice feeling, but it is more than that. Joy is God's miraculous life and strength. You have to have the joy of the Lord if you're going to make it through the trials and tribulations of this life. His joy will carry you supernaturally when you have no natural strength left.

The joy from praise can heal your mind and emotions too. It lifts depression and negativity right off of you. If you want to be happy you've got to learn to slip on the coat of praise and never take it off. The scriptural way of getting free of heaviness is to put on the garment of praise.

Praising God changes the spiritual atmosphere, which is why praise is a big part of our church service. We want His miraculous power to move in and change our lives. In the original Hebrew scriptures, if families did not go to Jerusalem to worship God at least once a year, He withheld the rain. Rain represents all the things of God: His presence, His power, His provision, His protection, His revelation, and His peace. We praise Him because we love Him, and then He pours water into the dry places and supernaturally transforms our lives. There's something about praise that brings happiness into your life. Happiness matters.

Praising God changes the spiritual atmosphere...

Praise No Matter How You Feel

Being a praiser means praising God whether you feel like it or not. We are commanded to praise at all times, to rejoice in the Lord always. This keeps your heart right with God and His blessings flowing into your life. As your praises go up to Him, His blessings come down to you. If you're in trouble, you praise your way out of it.

No matter who we are or what position we fill in the body of Christ, we all have to go through wilderness experiences. God took the children of Israel through the wilderness, the Holy Spirit led Jesus through the wilderness, and He will take us through the wilderness as well.

Wilderness experiences usually occur just before major promises are going to be fulfilled in your life. But you cannot go into your Promised Land until you praise Him in the desert. Part of your faith walk is learning to praise Him *before* you get the blessing and the victory. Your attitude must be, "No matter what happens, even if I never see the manifestation of the promise in this life, I will praise the Lord!"

God usually won't let you out of the wilderness until you learn to praise Him. That is because He is bringing you to a level of maturity that will be able to handle both the blessings and the challenges ahead of you.

You don't want to be thrown off your spiritual track with God when you get that new car, earn that promotion, buy that house, take that trip to the mission field, meet your mate and get married, and especially when you have children. All these things bring happiness, but they also bring responsibility.

Whether we are in the wilderness or in our Promised Land, whether we are high as a kite or low as a worm, we must praise the Lord. Praise is not an emotional issue. It is a faith issue. It is a maturity issue. We choose to praise Him with all of our heart, soul, mind, and strength at all times.

Hanging Out With Praisers

You cannot be a praiser of God and hang around critical and negative people. Some people only praise God when they are in church. They don't praise Him at all times and in all situations. They'll try to talk you out of praising the Lord and make it seem odd, unnecessary, and unimportant.

Sometimes in the wilderness, you are tempted to complain and get frustrated. The enemy will send people your way who resent being in the wilderness, have bad attitudes, and the last thing they want to do is praise God. If they come your way, you start moving the other way! When you're in the wilderness, you need to be around believers who praise God at all times.

If you attend a church that doesn't praise God—get out! That is not the place to be, especially if you need a breakthrough, a miracle, or just want to stay on track spiritually. You will never see a miracle in a praiseless church. They may have wonderful music that touches you, but the presence and power of God is not there because He inhabits the praises of His people.

You don't want to spend your time sharing your life with those who place no value on their relationship with

God. You want to be in a body of believers and hang out with those who praise God with all their heart, soul, mind and strength. Then, when you need a miracle, you will have some folk who can praise God and bring His power from heaven to earth.

God Is Looking for Praisers

God is looking for those who will worship Him in spirit and in truth. He's looking for those who will forget about themselves and praise Him without reservation. Praise is all about Him. He is looking for those who are tired of playing church and being religious, who will lose themselves in Him.

Real praise separates Christians from all other religions of the world. Religious people may sing or chant, but only those who have given their lives to the Lord can worship God in spirit and in truth. And we praise Him because He's given us something to celebrate. Jesus was dead, but now He's alive. His death and resurrection redeemed us from sin, hell, and eternal damnation!

Maybe folk are talking about you because they think you're a fanatic. They're calling you a fool behind your back. You may look foolish praising God in the middle of all your trouble, but their thinking will change when they see God turn your situation to your good in a miraculous way.

Jehosaphat looked pretty foolish sending a bunch of singers and musicians to the front of the battle. David looked foolish standing before Goliath with a little slingshot. Paul and Silas looked foolish praising God in shackles and chains. And Moses looked foolish with his rod pointed out over the Red Sea. But each one of them only looked foolish for a little while because the Red Sea parted, the shackles fell off, the giant tumbled to the ground, and Judah's enemies turned on themselves.

Sometimes believers judge the devotion and passion of other believers as foolishness. The woman with the alabaster box didn't shout at the top of her voice physically, but what she did sent shockwaves through Jesus' camp. The ointment in the box that she poured over Him was incredibly expensive. Some say it was worth a year's salary in those days, and the disciples criticized her for wasting so much money on a simple gesture.

That's what Jesus is looking for. He's looking for believers who pour their entire lives into Him, who continuously praise Him and worship Him in spirit and in truth with their whole hearts—no matter what they feel, what is happening in their lives, or who is talking about them. These are the ones whose hearts will be filled with His abundance of happiness. Remember, happiness matters. For more information contact **www.HeritageChristianCenter.com.**

Thought 17

HAPPINESS AND LETTING GO OF ANGER

The happiness of a man in this life does not consist in the absence but in the mastery of his passions.

Alfred Lord Tennyson

How you conduct yourself in life is either going to be conducive to happiness or sorrow? For example, you cannot wring your hands with worry, talk constantly about all the people who have done you wrong, and fly into fits of rage at the slightest sign of trouble—and live a happy life. After you come to the Lord, God wants to deal with the baggage of your past so that you can live a happy, fulfilled life. Happiness matters.

One of the main issues is anger. People don't meet our expectations, so we go off on them. Our children disobey and we yell at them (or worse). A traffic cop catches us speeding and we fume as he writes the ticket. By the time we go to bed at night, we are mad at the world and everybody in it.

Jesus will change all of that if you will let Him. As a branch is grafted into the vine, you are grafted into Him. All His strength and wisdom are available to you to put off that old angry person and put on the new patient, understanding, and forgiving you. With His help, you will not let the sun go down on your anger, and you will sleep in peace every night.

What Causes Anger?

Anger is nothing more than a byproduct of being hurt or disappointed. Anytime we perceive an injustice, that our rights are being violated, or that we are being treated unfairly, anger will rise up. If we think we are rejected because of our color, that our parents favored a brother or sister over us, or a friend talks about us behind our back, we deal with anger.

Anytime a person in a relationship does not meet our expectations we deal with anger, but we also deal with anger when it comes to our stuff. We lose our tempers when the car won't start, the television picture isn't just right, or the computer software we just installed doesn't do what it's supposed to do. When our lives depend on cell phones and laptops and Internet servers, we get furious when these things are out of order and our lives come to a halt.

It seems like everyone is mad about something today. We are mad in slow traffic. We are mad about unexpected bills. We easily get mad at our spouse and children because they are the closest to us and we expect them to meet our needs. And I don't think I have to say anything about getting angry with an ex-spouse!

Anger is about trying to gain or maintain control of something or someone

Maybe your mind keeps going back to the things that went wrong in your past. You are angry and bitter because you always got the leftovers and the secondhand clothes growing up, a relative got a college scholarship and excelled beyond you, and even God has let you down. You put your faith in Him and He didn't come through the way you thought He would come through.

Anytime your pride gets wounded, you can become angry. Pride will bring you down, and pride causes destruction in your life. Pride can get you so angry that you say and do terrible things, especially to those you really care about. Pride and control work together.

Anger is about trying to gain or maintain control of something or someone—a person, a conversation, a team project, a game, or a good night's sleep. That is why pride plays such a big part in anger issues. If you aren't willing to humble yourself and give up control to God—admit you have a problem, that you may not get your way, that you need help, or that you were wrong—you will not defeat anger in your life and find happiness and peace.

The control issue is right at the center of our salvation. We either let go and let God or we take matters into our own hands. Let me tell you how serious the control issue is. Witchcraft is about control. It is about self-will and manipulating other people to get what we want. Controllers are usually very angry people.

Sometimes we get angry at trivial things because we are not dealing with what is really bothering us. If we don't feel loved, we can become angry very easily. The slightest problem will set us off. Maybe that is why so many young people today are filled with rage. Busy, inattentive, and unaffectionate parents raise angry children who do not feel loved.

Then there is the overall pressure and stress of living in the world today. For most people, just trying to make a living and provide for their families has them on edge and they are easily angered.

Be Angry and Sin Not

Everybody gets angry, no matter who we are—rich, poor, old, young, educated, uneducated. Even when we love the

Lord anger is going to rise up in us, and God is serious about dealing with it the moment it rears its ugly head.

Jesus got angry many times with the religious folk, and one time He even turned over a few tables to make His point. But He didn't just trash the place in an uncontrolled rage and storm out. He explained to the people why He had run the moneychangers out of the temple and turned over their tables and chairs. He never used His anger as an excuse to operate in the flesh and hurt other people. He was always in complete control of His emotions.

Now that you love the Lord, you must learn to go to Him with your pressures and problems. The Bible says that those who wait upon the Lord shall renew their strength. You need God's strength to deal with your anger in the right way and keep from sinning.

Part of growing up in Christ means facing your past and overcoming it. By your past, I mean thirty years ago or thirty minutes ago. Some of us had a great upbringing but have been hit with some really disturbing and distressing situations recently. What I'm saying is that we should never stop turning to God for help and healing, no matter how many times He has helped us and healed us in the past.

Paul said that when he was a child he thought like a child, talked like a child, and acted like a child; but when he became a man, he put away those childish things. He grew up. That means trusting God, letting go of issues, forgiving others, not blaming other people for everything that goes wrong—and controlling your anger.

Anger will kill dreams and sabotage destinies.

One of the fruits of the Spirit is self-control. That means in Christ you have the supernatural ability to control your anger. When you get angry and upset, you can draw on His strength to deal with your emotions and figure out what is really bugging you—before you hurt yourself or someone else.

What Happens When Anger Turns to Sin?

When we give in to anger and operate in the flesh, we cause a multitude of problems and pain for ourselves and for anyone around us. Proverbs 29:22 says, "An angry man stirs up strife and a furious man abounds in sin." If you are full of anger you will sin, and sin always causes pain and destruction.

The Bible says that we should control our anger or else we literally give place to the enemy in our lives. When we lose our temper, we open the door for the powers of darkness to come in and cause heartache. Anger will kill dreams and sabotage destinies.

Anger hurts people and destroys relationships. When you get angry with somebody, communication and reasonable thinking stop. All you want to do is win your point, get your way, and crush your opponent. Anger pushes people away and causes deep division and distrust.

It seems as though there are many people today who are time bombs ready to explode. When anger is unrecognized and uncontrolled, the results can be devastating. Our jails and prisons are full of people who simply lost their tempers.

Anger also causes depression. Some people don't yell and throw things. Instead, they withdraw from life in total discouragement. Some become isolated and reclusive. If you continually fight depression, you probably have some unresolved anger issues.

I think you can see that anger plays a big role in the tragedies we experience in relationships, family life, our ministries and jobs, and even in the Church. Angry believers cause tremendous problems in the body of Christ. Maybe that's why the Bible has so much to say about controlling it.

The Wounded Heart

The real reason many people are angry all the time is because they are hurting and need healing. Anger is the fruit or manifestation of the pain that's in their hearts and minds. You can tell a wounded, angry person over and over how special they are and how much you love them, but they can't receive it. Their heart is so wounded that it is incapable of believing the truth.

Anger wears many different faces. Some people live in total silence, and behind that silence is sheer rage. For others it is sarcasm. Their anger is revealed through their smart mouth. Some people simply have a critical attitude all the time. Others express their anger by trying to control everyone and everything around them.

Here are a few questions that will help you to see if you are wounded and need to be healed and delivered from some baggage in your past.

- Are you moody?
- Do you sulk and pout if you don't get your way?
- Are you overly competitive, having to win at all costs?
- Do you yell when you're frustrated?
- Do you refuse to talk about what's bothering you?
- Do you raise your voice in a normal conversation?
- Do you hit or throw things?
- Do you say things in an argument that you regret later?
- Do you distrust people?
- Are you a loner?

- Have you built walls around yourself and push others away?
- Do you dislike yourself?
- Do you blame others for all of your problems?
- Do you see yourself as a victim?
- Do you hang up on people during phone conversations?
- Do you make excuses for your bad behavior, even for hurting others?

Is your family afraid of you? This is a tough one because if your family is really afraid of you, they probably are too afraid to tell you. But you've got to be able to ask your family, "Are you afraid of me?" That will tell you a whole lot about you.

The wounded person is the one who thinks that nobody could love somebody like them, and as a result they have a hard time getting along with other people. They also have a hard time believing God could love them, like them, or want to help them in any way. They can't trust anyone, including Him. The preacher says, "Trust God," and they can't figure out what that means.

Jesus said in Luke 4:18 that His mission was to heal the brokenhearted and those who had been bruised by life. But before He can heal you, you must admit you have a problem. If you can't admit that you have a wounded heart that is filled with pain, anger, and bitterness, then Jesus cannot heal you.

The answer is simple. What you need is love.

Again, your salvation is all about throwing off pride and humbling yourself before God. Once you humble yourself and admit you have been wounded and have an anger problem, then Jesus can begin the process of healing your heart. When you confess your sin of anger, tell God that you want to change your behavior, and open yourself up for His healing, delivering power; then He can come in and heal you and set your free.

All You Need Is Love

If you were deprived of love growing up, there is a very good chance that you look for love in all the wrong places right now. You may look for love in a crack pipe, a bar, a casino, one-night stand after one-night stand, work, or in food. Addictive behavior is a sign that somewhere in the depths of your soul, you haven't felt loved the way you want to be loved. And anger is always present because you hate the fact that you don't feel loved, you hate the addiction problem, and most of all you hate you.

The answer is simple. What you need is love. All of us need to be loved and to love others because God created us to love and be loved. If love is short-circuited in our lives in any way, we will be wounded and angry.

The only way we can feel truly loved is to be loved by God through Jesus Christ our Lord. But to receive His love means spending time with Him, opening up to Him, communicating our deepest desires and fears and frustrations to Him.

Then we need to listen to Him. We need to let Him show us the truth about our lives and in His Word so that we can get rid of our stinking thinking that is based on the enemy's lies. We need to receive His love and allow His truth to set us free. His love for us always neutralizes anger. His love and acceptance of us, no matter where we've been or what we've done, takes the sting out of our past and the anger out of our hearts.

Sometimes receiving God's love means humbling ourselves to other people! We also need to communicate honestly and openly with the significant people in our lives: our spouse, our children, our good friends, and our spiritual mothers and fathers. We have to be able to say, "Honey, I'm sorry that I hurt you." And sometimes we have to say, "Honey, let me tell you what you did that hurt me." When we humble ourselves and talk it through, we are not only receiving love; we are also loving others.

Proverbs 15:1 says that a soft answer turns away wrath, but a harsh word stirs up anger. Many times it's not what you say but how you say it that makes a difference. Sometimes you have to change your tone of voice, to be less demanding and more compliant. What I'm talking about is speaking the truth *in love*.

Love is the great neutralizer of nearly everything the enemy has to throw at you, and anger is a prime example of this. When you get angry with yourself or someone else, the first thing you do is become unloving. You blow up and scream, slam doors and anything else that opens and shuts, or become physically abusive to someone or something. Other more subtle ways are pouting and sulking, giving people the silent treatment, and ignoring or avoiding people. We express anger in different ways, but not in a loving manner!

When you commit yourself to walk in love at all times, you will overcome and defeat anger in your life. You will shut your mouth before speaking an unkind word, you will fold your arms before you strike something or someone, and you will look to the Lord for your salvation! Why? Because you choose to love the Lord, His people, and His creation more than you love yourself.

Choose to crucify your flesh and open your heart for the healing love of Jesus to flow through you. Then walk in the love of God and control your anger. Your heart will be glad and your life will be a much happier one. Happiness matters.

For more information contact:
www.HeritageChristianCenter.com.

Thought 18

CHANGING FOR HAPPINESS

If we don't change direction soon, we'll end up where we're going.

Professor Irwin Corey

Kiss the Past Good-bye!

You are where you are today and you are the person you are today because of what you have thought, spoken, and done in the past. If you want to be in a different place and be a better person tomorrow, then you have to make some changes in the way you think, speak, and act today. That usually means there are some things in your past that you have to deal with honestly.

One of the greatest examples of changing directions in life is the story, where Elijah the prophet met Elisha. Elisha was plowing with a dozen oxen when Elijah threw his mantle over his shoulders. This meant that Elijah was naming Elisha as his successor.

At first all Elijah could think of was saying good-bye to his parents, but then he sacrificed two of his oxen, fed everyone in the neighborhood, and left plowing forever. This illustrates to us that if we want to go to a new place in life, we must cut ties with our past, make some sacrifices, and bless those around us to get there.

Like Elijah, you need to kiss some things in your past good-bye. You may need to kiss the casino and the racetrack good-bye. You may need to kiss drinking and drugs good-bye. Or maybe you need to kiss that wrong relationship good-bye. And if those are the kinds of things you need to kiss good-bye, then the main thing you need to kiss good-bye is walking in your flesh instead of by the Spirit!

The Bible says that walking in the flesh brings death and walking in the Spirit brings life. It's time to decide that from this day on you will turn to Jesus for everything. That's how you walk in the Spirit and let God's life change your life.

The flesh is going to fight change because it wants to be in charge and get its way. We all can be stubborn and self-willed, and we all generally hate to be corrected! You cannot change without saying good-bye to your fleshly desires and letting Jesus be your Lord. Jesus has to be number one in your life, or you will never find true happiness. This principle of the kingdom of God is simple: When your life is all about you, you will be miserable; when it is all about Jesus, you will change and be happy.

Dealing with your past means putting Jesus in charge of your past, present, and future. He's the only one who understands you completely and knows how your life is supposed to go in order for you to be happy.

Only a crazy person will do the same thing year after year and expect to have different results or live in the past and expect to have a different future. How do you expect to be happy if you keep talking about What's-His-Name? How can you see a healthy future if you are holding onto crack and weed? It's time to release it all to God and receive His plan for your future.

The Bible says that God's plans are good plans. Jeremiah 29:11 says that His plans are for your good and not for evil, that when you plug into His plan for your life, you have great hope for your future. Right now you can have hope for your future if you will give it all to Jesus.

You've got to forget what lies behind and reach forward to what lies ahead. It's time for you to declare, "I will not stay stuck in the past. I'm kissing it all good-bye and surrendering completely to Jesus." You cannot change your past, but you can do something about your future.

It's time to let the Lord heal your wounds and get over all the things you've gone through. You're not the only one who has been molested, abused, abandoned, divorced, rejected, betrayed, or bankrupt. It is time to stop feeling sorry for yourself and get free of the bondage of your past. Quit carrying that heavy baggage and give it to Jesus. He's been waiting for you to let Him carry it away from you forever.

There's something else you need to know about your past. When you give it to Jesus and let Him heal you, He takes it and uses it for your good. Jesus will give you beauty for your ashes.

Adversity Brings Change

David made an interesting statement. He said, "It is good for me that I have been afflicted, that I may learn your statutes." Joseph said the same kind of thing, "But as for you, you meant evil against me; but God meant it for good, in order to bring it about as it is this day, to save many people alive."

Both of these great men of God knew what it was like to face adversity, to be on the Master Potter's wheel, and to endure the shaping and molding process. They knew that they had had to go through discomfort and difficulty and even pain in order to really understand God's Word and accomplish His vision for their lives.

There is a process you go through when you change. First, God will let you go through some fires in order to get your attention. If everything is going great in your life, you might not be listening to Him. But if all hell breaks loose, you will listen. David said that until he encountered some adversity, he had gone astray from the things of God.

When you stop praying, reading the Word, going to church, and fellowshipping with other believers, God will step back and allow some things in your life to get you back on track. Or it may just be time for you to make some changes, so God will allow adversity to come into your life and shake you up.

Once God has your attention, change can happen.

Once God has your attention, change can happen. As His child, you are supposed to change continually, always being transformed into the image of Jesus. If you stop the transformation process because you are distracted or deceived by the enemy or your flesh, you usually run into trouble. That's when you "come to yourself" like the prodigal son, and turn back to your heavenly Father. It is also when you take a good look at yourself and your life and ask Him what changes need to be made. You never want to be in that pit of pain again, so you ask Him to show you how you got there and how you can avoid winding up there in the future. Then you change.

When everything is nice, good, and sweet, you are usually not interested in change, and then you stop growing in God. When you stop growing in God you encounter problems, and those problems have a remarkable way of pointing out just what God wants you to change!

Now that God has your attention and has shown you what needs to be changed in your life, you must decide to obey Him and make the necessary sacrifices. Like Elisha, you will not move on in your calling without crucifying your flesh that ties you to your past.

You know that you will not get a breakthrough if you don't change what God is telling you to change. It could be something as simple—and as hard—as controlling your tongue, dealing with jealousy, or forgiving someone in your past. Or it could be spending more time with Him, volunteering in a ministry, or starting a new business.

When you obey the Lord in the midst of adversity and make the changes He has requested, you go to the next level in Him, and He prepares you for bigger and better things ahead. Trouble has a way of burning some things out of you that shouldn't be there and cannot be there when you get to where you are going next.

Being on the Master Potter's wheel isn't always comfortable or easy, but it's His way of maturing you, preparing you, transforming you, and bringing more happiness into your life.

Happiness matters.

Dealing With Change

In times of change we always have to remember that God never changes. That's why our focus has to be on

Him. He's the only thing we can count on at all times and in all situations because the world and everyone around us are constantly changing. God says that He is the Lord and He does not change. The Bible says that Jesus is the same yesterday, today, and forever. We can count on Him to be the rock of our salvation as we go through change.

Change can be a scary thing if you aren't walking with the Lord, but if you walk with Him change can become an exciting adventure. No matter how He changes your thinking and way of life, He is with you. Whatever you need to change, Jesus is the rock your life is built upon, the rock that wind and rain will not budge. He will provide everything you need and give you the courage and wisdom to make the changes He has asked you to make.

Elijah was God's man, and after he had prophesied to King Ahab that there would be no rain in Israel until he said so, God sustained him during the drought that followed. God told him to go to the brook Cherith, where he found running water, and He sent ravens with food for Elijah to eat. He provided everything Elijah needed during the famine. But when God was ready for Elijah to move into his next assignment, the brook dried up and the ravens stopped coming.

Has anything dried up and stopped producing in your life? That probably means that God is telling you that it is time for you to make some changes and move to the next assignment. Maybe you didn't even realize what a rut you had gotten into until the things that always satisfied you and took care of you stopped. That reminds you that God is your provider and protector and He changes not! He is the one who will provide for you and protect you in the next level just like He did in this one.

You don't have to fear change when you walk with the Lord.

You don't have to fear change when you walk with the Lord.

Although He often uses trouble as your ticket to promotion, you know He will be right beside you all the way. Jesus said He would never leave you or forsake you, that He would be with you until the end of the age—and that includes what you are going through right now.

You don't have to like your trouble, but you can have confidence that God will use that trouble to change your life and get you where He wants you to go. You are like a ship that has gone the same route, back and forth between two ports, for too long. One day a storm comes up and throws you off course, and you end up at a port you have never been to before.

None of us like it when the storms come against us, do we? But a storm causes us to change. It shakes up our thought patterns and causes us to consider new possibilities for our lives. Not only is the Lord with us, but also He blesses us in the storm in ways we never could have imagined before the storm.

Blessing Others in Changing Times

After Elisha said good-bye to his past and slaughtered his oxen, he fed the people around him. As you submit to the changes God is making in your life, He will use the very things He is commanding you to leave behind to bless those around you. This is one of the miracles of growing up in God. He takes even the worst things in your past and uses it for His glory and your good.

If you've been a drug addict and have allowed God to deliver you and heal you, you know how to talk to drug addicts. If you've been sexually or physically abused and Jesus has miraculously changed you from being a victim to a victor, you know how to pray for others who have been victims to become victorious.

The point I am making is that God uses the very things in our past that we are leaving behind to bless others as we go through change ourselves. The Bible says that we minister to others out of our own experience and pain, that as God encourages us we encourage others in the same way. He comforts us as we go through change, and then we comfort others as they go through similar changes.

When you go through change focusing on Jesus and not yourself, when change is all about Him and not you, He encourages you and leads you to other people who are going through the same kinds of change so that you can be an encouragement to them. Remember, it is more blessed to give than to receive. Even as God takes you through tremendous changes in your life, He blesses you by giving you the opportunity to encourage others. Happiness matters.

Nothing makes me happier than being able to minister to someone else and help him or her go through change because I have gone through or am going through the same change. Happiness floods my soul every time I share my testimony with someone and they receive the Lord or are delivered from the wounds and bondage of their past. Thank God I decided to change! And that makes me count it all joy when the next change comes. I know that as I submit to the changes God brings into my life, I will get stronger in Him, wiser in Him, and happier in Him, because happiness matters.

When our church membership was about one hundred people, we knew we had to make a change in order to grow. The Lord led us to start a program that we are still operating today, feeding hungry people. It wasn't long before we were running about three hundred members and change came again. We added other programs to minister to people and our membership grew to one thousand. With every change we made, we increased.

If you're fighting change you could be fighting God and shoving away your increase! Maybe it's time to get out of your comfort zone and change directions in your life. You won't truly be happy by staying in a rut and not growing, and in order to grow you have to change.

There is another thing you need to know about change. You don't have to wait for trouble to hit before you change. Ask the Lord right now what He wants to do in you and through you. Tell Him that you are ready and willing to change for Him. Change is the only way your life can be more productive and happy. Happiness matters.

If you are struggling with change contact us at
www.HeritageChristianCenter.com.

Thought 19

THE GUILT TRIP

Clearly, a civilization that feels guilty for everything it is and does will lack the energy and conviction to defend itself.

Jean Francois Revel

The Bible says that we have all sinned and fall short of the glory of God. That is why we feel guilty. The problem with feeling guilty is that it is impossible to fight the good fight of faith when we are feeling unworthy of God's blessing. As a result, we allow the enemy to paralyze us with shame and devastate our lives.

The guilt trip is not a pleasure ride! It is not God's will for His children, and it certainly does not promote happiness. If we are going to live happy lives, we must understand how to deal with guilt God's way and keep it out of our lives.

God's Purpose for Guilt

The dictionary defines guilt as "**1** the state of having done a wrong or committed an offense; culpability, legal or ethical **2** a painful feeling of self-reproach resulting from a belief that one has done something wrong or immoral **3** conduct that involves guilt; crime; sin."[1] Guilt is a state of knowing you've done wrong and deserve to be punished. That's why we go on a guilt trip. We punish ourselves or allow others to punish us because we believe we deserve to suffer for our failures.

In Galatians 3:24, Paul tells us that the law is a schoolmaster, or teacher, that leads us to Christ. The law teaches us that we are sinners in need of a savior. We cannot punish ourselves or have someone else punish us enough to pay the price for our sin. Someone needs to do it for us and bring us back to God. The Holy Spirit points to Jesus, who paid the debt for all of us on the cross, and then we receive Him as our Savior and Lord.

Paul also tells us that our sin nature remains in our flesh, even after we love the Lord. But our spirit has been transformed by the Holy Spirit. We are no longer dead to God. Now we are spiritually alive and connected to Him. We have this amazing understanding that something on the inside of us has changed forever from being inherently evil to inherently right with God.

When you give your life to the Lord, you know you are different. You know that the Spirit of God is on the inside of you. He bears witness that Jesus is in your heart. You know you are God's child and you will live with Him forever in heaven—and yet you are also aware of that old, sinful nature in your flesh that draws you to the same messes you were drawn to before you were born again. When you choose to act according to the flesh instead of your born again spirit and the Holy Spirit, you sin and guilt pours over you. You feel that you deserve to be punished. You have failed.

> *"A sinning man won't pray, and a praying man won't sin."*

Paul knew a lot about failures. He said, "I'm not doing what I want to do, but instead I'm doing the very thing I hate. I want to be good, but sometimes I do the very evil that I told God I wouldn't do. Inside I love God and want to do right. But I am constantly at war with my flesh on the outside, which wants to sin."

The Power to Choose Life

The flesh is always trying to take over. Jesus told us that our spirits are willing but our flesh is weak, so we need to pray to keep from falling into temptation. I love what

Darlene Bishop said, "A sinning man won't pray, and a praying man won't sin." As believers we have God's ability to say no to sin, but we have to stick close to Him or our flesh will take over again.

We have no strength in ourselves to say no to the sins we enjoyed in the past. That's why the Bible tells us to walk according to the Spirit and not the flesh. The flesh brings destruction and death into our lives but the Spirit brings life and peace. Sin may give us pleasure for a moment, but it will never make us happy.

Through the Blood of Jesus Christ we are changed and the Spirit of God lives inside us. Now we have His supernatural ability to say no to all the things that trapped us before we gave our lives to the Lord. But we have to choose to stay close to Him in order to walk in His overcoming power. That's why Paul exhorted us to pray without ceasing. We must stay close to God in order to say no to temptation and live a victorious, happy life. Happiness matters.

What happens when you blow it? You stop going to church to get built up in the Word of God, and you end up in sin? You can still choose life. God is still using guilt to draw you to Himself. But now there is a big difference. You know that Jesus took your punishment. You don't need to beat yourself up or have someone else beat you up in order to feel better about yourself. All you need to do is call on the name of the Lord, receive forgiveness, and get back to serving Him with your whole heart.

Now let me say this. You are forgiven and restored to fellowship with the Lord after you repent, but you may still have to bear the consequences of your failure. The Bible says that the way of the transgressor is hard because it is hard going to jail or going through a divorce. The consequences of sin are hard.

Although your mind will try to turn the consequences into a guilt trip, you don't have to let it. Instead, you can draw upon the grace and mercy of God to walk through those consequences humbly in peace, knowing that Jesus paid the eternal price for your sin and this too shall pass.

When you know that Jesus Christ took your punishment two thousand years ago, you realize that you don't have to punish yourself for your failures. When you realize that it's all under His Blood, you can refuse the guilt trip and choose life in Him instead.

The Accuser and The Convictor

Your spiritual enemy has a plan to steal your life and happiness by getting you to wallow in guilt, condemnation, and shame. If he can get you on a guilt trip, you won't feel worthy of the promises of God and your faith will be quenched. You won't pray or take authority over him, and he can run over you and destroy your life.

In Revelation 12:10-12 Satan is called the accuser of the brethren. It says that he stands before God and accuses us of all our sins day and night. It goes on to say that we overcome him by the Blood of the Lamb and the word of our testimony, and that we love God more than our own lives. This is a powerful statement! It says that we are continuously dealing with the accuser of the brethren, but we can defeat him every time by reminding ourselves and him that Jesus' Blood paid the price for our sin, we are children of God, and we love Him more than our own lives. Therefore, our spiritual enemy has no power over us. He cannot make us sin and he cannot make us go on a guilt trip for our past failures.

No matter who we are, we've all done things we regret. We've all had failures that are so bad we don't want anyone to know about them. One day we find ourselves doing what we told God we would never do again. The accuser of the brethren comes in and tells us that we are so dirty and ugly that God can't even look at us now. But let me tell you the good news.

The truth is, before you ever fail, the Holy Spirit is already convicting you that what you are considering is wrong. He says ever so gently and lovingly that you are about to go the wrong direction, away from God. Then, if you still sin, He is there to continue convicting you that you have sinned and need to come back to God to be forgiven and restored. Remember this: If sin didn't bother you, you wouldn't be saved. The very fact that you feel guilt over sin means you are God's child!

If you can sin and it doesn't mean a thing to you—you can just blow it off and not care—then you need to give your life to the Lord. You know you are on your way to heaven when you are disgusted with yourself and you fall short.

Remember this: If sin didn't bother you, you wouldn't be saved.

As a believer, you are appalled when you fail. This is where you need to be very careful to listen to the conviction of the Holy Spirit instead of the accusations of the enemy. If you listen to the enemy, you will go on a guilt trip because he will make you feel like a total loser. But if you listen to the Holy Spirit, you will come back into fellowship with God because He loves you and forgives you. Instead of going on a guilt trip, you will be restored and joy will return. Happiness matters.

The enemy is always telling believers, "Okay, you have really done it this time. You have crossed the line. You cannot go back to God. You have committed the unpardonable sin and are lost forever." First of all, the unpardonable sin is simply not receiving Jesus Christ as your Lord and Savior. That is it! All other sins are forgiven through the Blood of Jesus.

Romans 8:1 says there is no condemnation for those who are in Christ Jesus. That means no more guilt trips. The Holy Spirit convicts to bring you home; the accuser of the brethren condemns to put you on a fruitless guilt trip. The next time you mess up or fail, refuse to listen to the accuser and instead listen to the convictor. Then your happiness will be restored. Happiness matters.

Come Boldly to the Throne of Grace

In the original Hebrew scriptures, the high priest went through an elaborate ceremony for the forgiveness of trespasses. He would take a spotless lamb, sacrifice it, and put its blood on the tip of his right ear, the tip of his right thumb, and the tip of his big toe on his right foot. This symbolized that the blood of the Lamb cleansed them from all the sin they had in their hearts, put their hands to, or walked in.

After the high priest cleansed himself and the nation of Israel, he would enter the Holy of Holies and sprinkle the blood of the Lamb on God's mercy seat. The blood was the atonement for the sins of all. When the high priest came out of the Holy of Holies, everyone was relieved that their sins were covered for another year and God would hear their prayers. The blood of the lamb gave the children of Israel full access to God.

Before the blood was applied, the children of God were afraid of His judgment. But after the blood was applied they could boldly come to His throne of grace to receive mercy. In other words, the blood made them worthy. They knew they weren't worthy in themselves, but the blood made them worthy.

God tells us that Jesus is our High Priest, who took His own Blood into the Holy of Holies in heaven and sprinkled it on God's real mercy seat. Because of what Jesus has already done, we can boldly come to His throne of grace and receive mercy in our time of need. His Blood makes us worthy to have full access to God, enjoying His presence and power in our lives.

The Blood of Jesus Christ lets us know that God isn't mad at us! He is not sitting in heaven just waiting for us to mess up so that He can hit us with a lightning bolt or strike us with cancer. He loves us so much that He sent His only begotten Son to die for us. He doesn't want to punish us for sin; He wants to help us get out of sin!

Make no mistake, no matter how good a Christian you are, there will come a time where you will fail God in some way. But that is your signal to get closer to God, not to run away from Him. The Blood of Jesus Christ still satisfies Him today! He cannot be angry with you when you sin because all He sees is Jesus' Blood. Instead of going on a guilt trip, run to the Father! Come to the throne of grace to obtain mercy.

Make the Love Choice

I've let the Lord down more times than I want to remember. But I keep on repenting, and He keeps on forgiving. Then I look in the Bible and see all the people Jesus forgave. The woman at the well had had five husbands and was just living with a man, yet Jesus ministered to her and saved her. When the religious Jews threw the woman caught in adultery at Jesus feet, He didn't condemn her. He loved her and told her not to sin anymore.

Peter ran from Jesus when he denied Him three times, but Jesus appeared to him after the resurrection and talked about love, not judgment. He said, "If you love Me, feed my sheep." In other words, "Peter, if you love Me, get out there and do what I've called you to do. Stop wallowing in guilt and letting the accuser keep you from ministering. My Blood has cleansed you from all unrighteousness!"

No sin is too great for the Blood of Jesus to wash away except rejecting His Blood. No sin is beyond the forgiveness of our loving God except rejecting Jesus as Lord and Savior. If you have received Jesus as your Lord and Savior, then you are forgiven—past, present, and future—and are free from all guilt.

Religion threatens you with judgment and condemns you if you sin; it will put you on a continual guilt trip. But a relationship with God through the shed Blood and love of Jesus Christ motivates you to live right because He loves you and you love Him. The reality of God's love, forgiveness, and acceptance does not give you a license to sin; it gives you a reason not to sin! You choose not to sin because you love Him, not because you are afraid He will make you sick or kill your children.

Declare today that you are no longer on a guilt trip.

You must stay in fellowship with God and with other believers if you want to stay free of guilt. It's hard to go on a guilt trip when you have a group of Christian friends who keep reminding you how much God loves you and forgives you, who love you and forgive you when you mess up. Don't let the accuser of the brethren separate you from the saints just because you mess up! The Bible says we should confess our faults to one another so we can be healed from the guilt and consequences of our sin. We need one another.

Declare today that you are no longer on a guilt trip. From this day forward you are happily on a love trip with Jesus and the body of Christ! You can be happy if you get your past behind you through a relationship with Jesus

Christ. Happiness matters. If you need further assistance contact us at www.HeritageChristianCenter.com.

Thought 20

HAPPINESS AND LETTING GO OF THE PAST

A man must be big enough to admit his mistakes, smart enough to profit from them, and strong enough to correct them.

John C. Maxwell

The main point God makes to us again and again is that we should not hold onto the past. Paul says that, forgetting the past, he presses on toward the fulfillment of his calling in God. We are to go forward trusting Him, no matter what already has taken place in our lives. We need to let go of the past and move forward in the present to fulfill our destiny in the future.

Remember Not, Consider Not

In the original Hebrew Scriptures, the prophet Isaiah writes, "Do not remember the former things, nor consider the things of old. Behold, I will do a new thing, now it shall spring forth; shall you not know it? I will even make a road in the wilderness and rivers in the desert". When God says to remember not the former things, He is telling us how to be happy and successful. He's telling us to stop thinking about all the failures of the past, and trust God to start over.

People who live in the past are sad.

People who live in the past are sad. When you're around them you almost feel like they are dead. All they can talk about is their past lives, good or bad. Some people who idolize their past think and talk about the glory days. But they have no life in the present and are cutting off their future by staying stuck in their past. You'll never be happy if you live in the past. Happiness matters.

Some people get stuck in their past in a really bad way. Their whole life is a wilderness because they cannot let go of the wounds and hurts that took place years ago. Sometimes these are childhood experiences that were traumatic and overwhelming to them then and continue to overshadow their lives now. Sometimes terrible things happened to them as adults, and they have never recovered from the loss, the shock, and the horror of what took place.

I believe God wants us to deal with our past and move on. Usually we deal with it as we move on. But we need to get past it because God is always doing a new thing. He is into change! He is a God of multiplication and growth, a master builder. Although He doesn't change, everything around us is continuously changing.

God said, "I want to bring a river in your wilderness." He wants to build your life into something magnificent, so that rivers of life flow out of your innermost being. If you feel like your life is dry, God said it could be because you are still holding on to the past. Everything in the present just reminds you of what happened before, and He wants to water the desert of your life so that you can bring the healing waters of His Word and Spirit to others.

God says to remember not the former things; neither consider the things of old because He wants to do something new in our lives. He wants us to quit looking back over the past and begin to make some new plans for our future. As long as we are living in the past we are not going to be going forward, and we are not going to be happy. Happiness matters.

What If?

Maybe you wish you could turn the clock back and correct your mistakes. You want to get into one of those time machines, go back, and change the decisions you made earlier in your life. You think, *What if I had married somebody else? What if I had taken that other job? What if I had gone to school? What if I had gone into the military?* You've got all of these what ifs spinning around in your head, and you can't hear what God is trying to say to you about today and tomorrow.

Maybe you feel helpless because your past is so dark and frightening that it casts a shadow over today and points to a very bleak tomorrow. Your what ifs are a little more serious. *What if I had been born into a nice family? What if I had both a mother and a father and they never beat me? What if I never had any uncles or aunts who abused me sexually? What if my brother never got shot and killed in the gangs?*

All I can tell you is what God says in His Word. You can't change the past. What's done is done. But He can heal you of all the pain, rejection, and abuse in your past. He is in the restoration business. He restores souls. So you need to let Him restore your soul and stop looking back.

You can't change your past, but you can change yourself right now. You can open up your heart and mind to Jesus and let the Great Physician go to work on you. Don't let the past cripple you from walking into your future! Instead of thinking, *What if that hadn't happened?* Begin thinking, *What if I trust Jesus and get healed of all that stuff? What if I put my hand in His and take a step forward? What if I walk out of my past and into my future with Jesus?*

Don't Turn Into a Pillar of Salt!

The clock will be stopped in your life until you stop looking back. In Luke 17:32 Jesus told us to remember Lot's wife. God miraculously preserved Lot and his wife and daughters. Sodom and Gomorrah were about to be destroyed, so He sent a couple of angels in to rescue them. The angels told Lot and his family, "Okay, in a minute this whole place and everyone in it is going up in smoke, so just follow us and we will get you out of town. One thing, though, after you leave, don't look back."

Lot and his family were living in the worst sin city in history. It was so bad that when the angels came to their house, the men in the city wanted to have sex with them! That's why the angels said, "We know you don't want to be here, and God has sent us to take you to a new place. In fact, you're going to a new level in God. And the first thing you need to do is to not look back because that is not your future. Your future is with God in a much better place."

Jesus said, "Remember Lot's wife," because she looked back and turned into a pillar of salt. She refused to obey the Word of the Lord given to her by the angels, and she refused to leave the sins and horrors of her past behind her. As a pillar of salt, she was a monument of someone who rejected God's will. His will was for her to leave the past behind and be salt and light to a dying world. But she could not let go of the past and became a monument of what could have been.

No believer can live much of a life or serve God well if they constantly look over their shoulder and think about their past. You need to make up your mind to stop looking back and determine in your heart that you will walk with Him into the great future He has prepared for you.

Keep Moving Forward

Once you put the past behind you and begin to move forward, there are a whole lot of things that can happen. Some people are excited that they are finally out of their rut, they are feeling better about themselves, and they are having new adventures in the Lord.

But it isn't long before the going gets tough, however, and that's when we are all tempted to look back and desire that former relationship or previous job. When we hit obstacles and challenges, that's when we remember the former things and, like the children of Israel, want to go back to Egypt. "Man, some of these Christians can be really mean. At least when I was drunk or stoned everyone loved me."

If you haven't figured it out yet, the enemy is really a liar! He will step in and oppose everything God is doing in your life. He will pervert God's Word and entice you to sin, just like he did to Eve in the Garden. Nothing's changed since Eden. God is still the good guy. The enemy is still the bad guy. God wants you to forget the past and go forward. Your spiritual enemy wants you to get stuck in a rut and die in the mud.

No matter what happens or who says what, keep moving forward with the Lord. Trust Him. Don't listen to the lies of the enemy. It was not that great back there or you wouldn't have changed directions in the first place! There is nothing in the past that will make you happy in the future.

No matter what happens or who says what, keep moving forward with the Lord.

The Blame Game

If you want Jesus to look you in the eye and say, "Well done! You are a good and faithful servant," you must take responsibility for your life. You must stop blaming others. It's time to quit blaming your boss. It's time to quit blaming the white man, the black man, and any other color or culture that you have stereotyped because some of them treated you or your loved ones badly.

It's time to stop blaming your parents. What a waste of time to sit in bitterness because of what your daddy or mama did or didn't do. It's over. You are the adult now, and you can change things. Don't waste your breath complaining about your terrible upbringing. Change yourself and your kids will have a better upbringing than you did.

Maybe you need to stop blaming yourself. It's time to quit beating yourself up over your past failures. Everyone makes a bad decision from time to time. And guess what? You might even make a few today and in the future. Making mistakes and going through failure is part of the learning process in life. Sometimes we don't know the right way of doing something until we do it the wrong way. And God always redeems the time and works everything for our good.

The enemy's plan is to make you think that God is mad at you, that you have committed the unpardonable sin. But the only unpardonable sin is to reject Jesus Christ as the Lord of your life. If he can't convince you that you've committed the unpardonable sin, the enemy will whisper in your ear, "You've gone too far this time. You will go to heaven, but God can't use you anymore."

No matter what you've done, God is not mad at you. The only reason He might be grieved is because you have strayed away from Him and He wants you to come home! He is waiting with open arms. The Bible says that if you confess your sin, He is faithful to forgive you and cleanse you from all unrighteousness. His mercies are new every morning. You can start a new life every day with the Lord, so get over it! He wants you to forgive yourself and go on.

I want you to know that it doesn't matter what people say about you because of your past. Once you repent, receive forgiveness, and are washed clean by the Blood of Jesus, your slate is clean. Your past is washed away into the sea of forgetfulness and, although people may choose to remember your past, God chooses to forget it. In His eyes you are brand new, dressed in a robe of righteousness, and fully prepared to serve Him. That is all He sees and that is all you should see.

The Power of God's Grace

The reason the enemy keeps throwing your past in your face is because he is afraid of where you're going. He will remind you that one mistake can affect your entire life. One mistake can leave you hurting for years, full of regret and depressed. One mistake can cause the breakup of your marriage and family. One mistake can cost you everything financially. One mistake can destroy your ministry. One mistake can put you in prison. One mistake can cause you tremendous embarrassment. But the Blood of Jesus is greater than any mistake you have made in your past or will make in your future, and nothing is impossible to you if you only believe.

God's grace, His favor that you can never earn but He gives freely, is not only sufficient for you to go through fire and flood. His grace is also your strength, your wisdom, and your hope for the future. Folk may want you to be punished, but God's grace wants you to forgive and forget to let go of the past and go forward with Him. People may be through with you, but God is never through with you.

People can get tired of you messing up and throw you aside, but God is patient and kind. He loves you and knows you have a heart after Him. He will stick with you if you just stick with Him and keep moving forward in faith. You cannot change your past. But He can use it for your good if you will trust Him.

Do you have some skeletons in your closet? Everybody does. Some of them are uglier than others, but we all have a past.

All of us need to close the chapters in our lives that have already taken place and let God write some new ones. But it is hard for Him to lead us into the future when our transmission is stuck in reverse and we're obsessed with our rear-view mirror! He says, "Quit driving past her house. Quit playing 'our song.' Quit putting your life on hold waiting for someone or something to ride out of your past and save you. Let go of the past and let God do a new thing.

You will be so much happier when you let go of your past! Happiness matters. For further help contact us at www.HeritageChristianCenter.com.

Thought 21

SEVEN SECRETS TO HAPPINESS

Life's greatest happiness is to be convinced we are loved.

Victor Hugo

God looks at you and sees something beautiful. It doesn't matter whether you are fat or skinny or are having a good or bad hair day. He thinks you are the most gifted, talented, delightful person, whether you play spoons or a concerto on the violin. He can't wait until you wake up every morning so you can go on adventures of faith with Him, and when you sleep at night He lovingly watches over you.

He sets His mighty angels around you day and night to guard you and minister to you when you need it. He loves it when you pour out your heart to Him and allow Him to heal you and transform you into the image of His Son. No one wants you to be happy more than God does. He sent His Son to die for you so you could be happy. He also gave you His Word to show you how to be happy. In this last chapter, we are going to review some of the things we've talked about in the previous chapters. But this time we are going to really see them through the eyes of His love for us, our love for Him, and our love for each other.

The Sermon on the Mount Tells You How to Be Happy

The Sermon on the Mount is grounded in what Jesus called the new commandments: Love God with all your heart, soul, mind, and strength; and love your neighbor as yourself. Happiness is loving God, yourself, and His people.

These principles reveal seven secrets of getting happy and staying happy in our daily lives. Happiness matters.

1. In Matthew 5:16 Jesus said to let your light shine. Now that you know how much God loves you and you love Him, you can show His love to your family, your co-workers, your friends, your neighbors, and anyone you meet. You can be so consumed with loving others as God loves you that you forget to be angry, sad, or afraid! Happiness matters.

On the practical side, nearly every Bible-believing church has a class on how to share your faith. Taking these classes will give you even more confidence and wisdom to go out and be a witness for the Lord. There is no greater joy than telling others about the difference Jesus has made in your life—unless it is leading someone else to Him!

2. In Matthew 5:22 Jesus said to control your anger. If you live in America today, you live in an angry society, and I don't think it is too much better in other countries of the world. You get behind the wheel of a car and people get mad at anyone who gets in front of them. Even when someone we love irritates us we can fly into a rage. I have devoted a whole chapter on anger because believers still have a problem with it.

Jesus knew that you couldn't be happy if you are angry all the time. Paul wrote that anger was not a bad thing unless you used it as an excuse to operate in the flesh, like lose your temper, hit someone, or destroy someone's property. In other words, anger can rise up in you for a just reason, but don't allow that anger to get out of control. And He said you shouldn't let the sun go down without resolving it.

Life brings many opportunities to get angry. You are going to get angry with your spouse, you kids, your boss, and even your pastor now and then; but do not go to bed until you have prayed about it and talked it out if you need to do so. Sometimes we get angry, pray about it, God shows us something we didn't know, and our whole perspective changes. We go to bed in peace, wiser than before. Other times we need to call someone, sit down with someone, or take someone aside to resolve a conflict. But don't do anything until you pray and get God's wisdom.

When anger is uncontrolled the results can be devastating. Our prisons are full of people who did not control their anger and did something they regret. But when you sit down with God and find out what's really making you mad and how you need to deal with it, anger can be a stepping-stone to greater wisdom, understanding, and joy. Control your anger and be happy. Happiness matters.

3. In Matthew 5:23-24 Jesus tells you to restore broken relationships. Relationships change, and that is not always bad. Sometimes they are not broken; they are just inactive. Both parties are fine with each other, but they have moved on into other phases of their walk with the Lord and are not as close as they were in the last phase. If they see each other, it is like they pick up right where they left off, as though they had never been apart. Then they continue on in the knowledge that they have a loving friend forever.

Other relationships are a lot more work. Someone misunderstands and gets mad. Someone has a difficult day and takes it out on another person. Someone sins and feels guilty and doesn't want to be around anyone, especially you. Then there are those who simply do not want to restore their relationship with you, and there is nothing you can do to change their mind. Nevertheless, Jesus wants you to do your best. Then, the burden is off of you.

> *Walking in forgiveness is the way to live a happy life, and happiness matters.*

Don't let a broken relationship cause you to go off by yourself and be isolated. Loners are not happy because God created you to be with people. That's why one of the chapters in this book is about being a people person. It is vital that you know how to get along with people to be happy—and sane. Every serial killer and deranged psychopath on the planet was a loner! We all need friends and family to encourage us and keep us on the right track with God.

In order to be restored, most broken relationships require forgiveness. If you are going to be happy in this life, you'll have to forgive folk you don't want to forgive; and eventually you will rejoice in that. When you forgive everyone of everything, whether you feel like it or not, you are being just like Jesus. Walking in forgiveness is the way to live a happy life, and happiness matters.

That means forgiving people who hurt you and people who made you mad. It means forgiving everyone from the man who molested you as a child to the person who just took your parking space. You cannot afford to have unforgiveness in your life. And whenever possible and appropriate, go to that person and make things right between you.

You used to spend Thanksgiving with Uncle Leroy every year, but one year you got mad at him. You just realized you haven't talked to him for two years—and you know that's not just a coincidence. It's time to pray and ask the Lord to show you what to do to restore that broken relationship.

One thing I have learned is that a major offense will come against you just before God promotes you. When you are deeply offended by something or someone, make the decision to deal with it properly so that God can get you where He wants you to go. He cannot promote babies who won't do their best to restore a broken relationship.

4. In Matthew 5:27-28 Jesus said to avoid sexual sin. We live in a sex-crazy society today. Movies, television, magazines, advertising, and even billboards are sexually explicit. Jesus said we shouldn't even think about such things. Paul said we are not to be like the people of this world. We are to run from all lust of the flesh by not even thinking about it.

Some time ago I took an anonymous poll in our church. I asked the people to identify the two top sins in their lives. Most of them answered lack of tithing and sexual sin.

Everything around you is trying to destroy you through sexual sin, and sometimes you have no idea where it is going to come from. The enemy works overtime on this one because it appeals to you if you are lonely, angry, jealous, or wounded. He knows that if he can get you to fall into sexual sin, he can devastate you and those closest to you, especially if you are married and have children.

> *God's greatest treasure is His children...*

Sometimes people will get so hooked into sexual sin that they forfeit their destiny in God. This is serious business! It all comes back to love. To overcome any sin, but especially sexual sin, you have to love Jesus more than a moment of pleasure. Sexual sin will give you a short time of pleasure, but loving Jesus will give you a lifetime of happiness.

5. In Matthew 6:19 Jesus said not to lay up treasures here on earth but to lay up treasures in heaven. You cannot take money to heaven. There is only one thing you can take to heaven, and that is people. God's greatest treasure is His children, and when you lead someone to the Lord and they become His child, you add to God's treasure and your eternal reward.

One reason God commanded us to give generously, is so money would not become an idol, something we look to more than God for security and happiness. In Matthew 6:24 Jesus said that we cannot serve God and money. If you say you love God and don't give to Him first in your finances, you are dealing with idolatry. You are putting more faith and trust in money than you are in God.

God wants us to be prosperous, but not at the expense of our relationship with Him. Third John 1:2 says that He wants us to prosper as our soul prospers. Our soul will not prosper without putting Him first in all areas of our lives. He wants to be our source of security and happiness because no one loves us like He does.

I know from personal experience that if you put the Lord first in everything, He will bless you and see that your needs are met. He wants to teach you to be a giver. He wants you to be like Him and think of others before yourself. The enemy and the materialistic world you live in will tempt you to be greedy and selfish, but that will never make you happy. God knows that the only way you will be happy is to give because it is more blessed to give than to receive.

When you love God and you love others as yourself, it is not hard to give cheerfully. And the more you give to God's people and fund the work of the ministry, the more souls come into the kingdom, which means more treasure in heaven!

6. In Matthew 6:25 Jesus said to stop worrying about the future. Other than what the Bible prophesies, we don't know for sure what the future holds. So it's really easy to start worrying about it if we don't keep our eyes on the Lord and trust Him with all our heart. That's the only way we can stop worrying and be happy. Happiness matters.

God's Word tells you that He will keep those in perfect peace whose mind is stayed on Him. You can have peace in the middle of every storm if you quit worrying about it and say, "God, I put this in Your hands. I trust You."

The enemy's plan is to make you believe that the problems you are having today will never get any better. He wants you to look around you, listen to the news on television, and hear all the horror stories and tragedies in other people's lives. Why? He wants you to literally worry yourself to death.

In the chapter on worry, we saw how it will kill your faith and your joy. But we also learned that Jesus, the Prince of Peace, is the antidote for worry. If we trust in Him for our future, knowing that He has everything under control and will work all things for our good, worry cannot steal our happiness.

You know your future is secure because you are secure in the One who holds it in His hands. His love for you assures you that you have a great future ahead of you.

7. In Matthew 7:1-3 Jesus said to stop judging others. Judging another person will bring the same judgment on you because of God's law of sowing and reaping. If you plant judgment you will reap judgment. The way you treat others is the way you will be treated. God is so serious about love that His kingdom runs on the law of love.

If you judge others, you will never be happy. It's the nature of the flesh to be judgmental, so we all are tempted to do it from time to time. Sometimes we are so shocked by something someone does, we judge him or her and don't even realize it. Sometimes we just get on our high horse of self-righteous indignation and judge people. Either way, we need to stop it and return to walking in love instead of condemnation.

Judgmental people are not happy because they are reaping what they sow. If you realize you are being judgmental, stop and repent. Get with Jesus and forgive and let it go. Then some day when you make a mistake or are overtaken by a fault, the people around you will be compassionate instead of condemning.

Anytime you are judgmental toward others, you are telling God to get off His throne so you can take over. You must learn to leave the judging to God, and love your fellow man as He loves you. He loves you no matter what you think, say, or do. Then He expects you to turn around and love others the same way.

God takes it very personally when you don't walk in love towards others. That is why He set the law of sowing and reaping in motion, so that you and I would know that if we did not walk in love, those around us would not walk in love toward us.

Jesus was incredibly popular with the masses of people because He walked in love toward them. They were used to having the religious leaders tell them what to do and what not to do, and if they didn't do right they were condemned and punished. When Jesus came along and just started loving them, healing them, and delivering them, He was like rivers of water in a dry desert to them. They hung on every word He spoke and didn't want to sin anymore because they knew He loved them. When He said, "Go and sin no more," they did not want to go out and sin against the One who loved them and had set them free.

> *God takes it very personally when you don't walk in love towards others.*

You will be happy when you commit your life to walk in love like Jesus walks in love. All of the miracles, healings, deliverances, and signs and wonders He performed were motivated by love. Even His wrath against sin and evil is a facet of His love! He has a righteous rage against anything that is not pure and holy and loving because it brings nothing but pain and destruction into your life.

If you can obey what Jesus said and love, not only will happiness come into your life and stay in your life, but it will spill over into the lives of everyone you touch. And making someone else happy is the greatest happiness of all. Happiness matters. If you need encouragement contact us at www.HeritageChristianCenter.com.

ENDNOTES

Introduction

1. http://www.m-w.com/dictionary/happiness

Thought 1: Hakuna Matata—Don't Worry, Be Happy!

1. Erma Bombeck, *God's Little Devotional Book for Mothers*

Thought 4: Praise Your Way to Happiness

1. James Strong, *Exhaustive Concordance of the Bible*, "Hebrew and Chaldee Dictionary," (Nashville, TN: Thomas Nelson Publishers, 1984), #1984, #3050.
2. *Webster's New World College Dictionary*, Third Edition, Victoria Neufeldt, Editor-in-Chief (New York: Macmillan, Inc., 1996), p. 1479.

Thought 12: Depression and Happiness

1. *Webster's New World College Dictionary*, Third Edition, p. 371.

Thought 14: The Guilt Trip

1. *Webster's New World College Dictionary*, Third Edition, p. 600.

Thought 15: Fear Steals Happiness

1. James Strong, *Exhaustive Concordance of the Bible*, "Hebrew and Chaldee Dictionary," #3374.
2. Spiros Zhodiates, *The Complete Word Study Dictionary: New Testament*, (Chattanooga, TN: AMG Publishers, 1992,) #5401.

Thought 16: Eight Positive Attitudes

1. Spiros Zhodiates, *The Complete Word Study Dictionary: New Testament*, (Chattanooga, TN: AMG Publishers, 1992,) #4239, #4236.

PRAYER OF SALVATION

God loves you…no matter who you are, no matter what your past. God loves you so much that He gave His only begotten Son for you. The Bible tells us "…whoever believes in Him shall not perish but have eternal life" (John 3:16, NIV).

Jesus laid down His life so that we could spend eternity with Him in heaven and experience His absolute best on earth. If you would like to receive Jesus Christ as your Lord and Savior, say the following prayer out loud and mean it from your heart.

Heavenly Father, I come to You admitting that I am a sinner. Right now, I choose to turn away from sin, and I ask You to cleanse me from all unrighteousness. I believe that Your Son, Jesus, died on the cross to take away my sins. I also believe that He rose again from the dead so that I might be forgiven of my sins and made righteous through faith in Him. I call upon the name of Jesus to be the Lord and Savior of my life. Jesus, I choose to follow You and ask that You fill me with the power of the Holy Spirit. I declare right now that I am a child of God. I am free from sin and full of the righteousness of God. I am on my way to heaven in Jesus' name. Amen.

ALSO BY DENNIS LEONARD

WHAT MEN NEED TO KNOW ABOUT WOMEN

What do women want? It's a question men have been asking since Eve joined Adam in the Garden of Eden. Why do they always want to "talk"? Why do they constantly seek affirmation? What about that "submission" issue? And how can you help the woman in your life fulfill her hopes and dreams and become all God created her to be?

These aren't simple questions … as you know!

But Dennis Leonard has filled the pages of this comprehensive book with solid biblical principles that cut straight to the core of that often illusive relationship between men and women. These are principles you will want to read again and again as you take the hand of the woman you love and walk together in your calling as joint heirs of the grace of life.

ISBN: 1-880809-51-6

YOUR BEST DAYS ARE STILL AHEAD

Your Best Days Are Still Ahead reveals powerful principles that release you to walk in the freedom that belongs to you as a child of God. There are no shortcuts to freedom, but there is a way of escape. It's time to move beyond your self-imposed boundaries. Learn how you can break free from the past and master the keys to your future.

ISBN: 1-880809-53-2

KEYS TO FINANCIAL FREEDOM

Financial insecurity is the #1 cause of stress, loss and breakdown in families and relationships today. Many people want to be blessed. They want to have more than enough, but few are willing to pay the price. Financial freedom is a choice. Learn how to assess your financial condition, learn new money management habits, how to build a financial plan and how to grow in wealth and prosperity.

ISBN: 1-880809-20-6

DON'T JUDGE MY FUTURE BY MY PAST

You cannot change where you have been, but you can change where you are going. Don't Judge My Future By My Past offers encouragement and hope for everyone held back by their past. God loves us and has a future full of hope reserved for each of us. No matter what our past, with God's help we can put it behind us and move into a future brighter than anything we have ever imagined.

ISBN: 1-880809-15-X

FAILURE IS NOT THE END

This book is solid and carefully targeted Bible-based discipleship framed in a 30-day "life makeover" plan to help you overcome your past and step into your God-ordained destiny. It will help you make strategic and biblical course corrections that will set you on track for the journey of pursuing your life's purpose.

ISBN: 1-880809-43-5

www.HeritageChristianCenter.com

You can order additional copies of this book along with other titles and helpful ministry tools by Dennis Leonard by logging onto the following website:

www.HeritageChristianCenter.com

Or by writing or calling:

Dennis Leonard Ministries
9495 East Florida Avenue
Denver, Colorado 80247

(303) 369-8514